"In this seminal book, Fanny Brewster contributes to the individuation of Analytical Psychology into the 21st century from her lived personal and professional experience."
—**Alan G. Vaughan, Ph.D., JD, Jungian analyst, author of** *The African Diaspora: Post Modern Views of Jung and Analytical Psychology in Cultural Context*

"Dr. Brewster's book is certainly a milestone in Jungian literature, addressing a difficult and inadequately explored area of Jung's work regarding indigenous peoples and American people of color."
—**Joseph R. Lee, Jungian analyst; President of The Philadelphia Society of Jungian Analysts**

"Within the social construct of race, the first language we learn is the language of silence, but this book breaks that silence."
—**Eugene Ellis, MA, Dip, IATE. PSA accredited, UKCP registered Integrative Arts Psychotherapist**

"In Dr. Brewster's writing, the flaws in Jung's thinking become a rich vein of exploration."
—**William Allured, Ph.D., Brookhaven Institute, USA**

"Fanny Brewster's *The Racial Complex* is a major contribution to the understanding of the most corrosive and destructive cultural complex in American history that continues to be an unending source of great suffering in America today."
—**Thomas Singer, MD, co-editor of The Cultural Complex**

THE RACIAL COMPLEX

In *The Racial Complex: A Jungian Perspective on Culture and Race*, Fanny Brewster revisits and examines Jung's classical writing on the theory of complexes, relating it directly to race in modern society. In this groundbreaking exploration, Brewster deepens Jung's minimalist writing regarding the cultural complexes of American blacks and whites by identifying and re-defining a psychological complex related to ethnicity.

Original and insightful, this book provides a close reading of Jung's complexes theory with an Africanist perspective on raciality and white/black racial relationships. Brewster explores how racial complexes influence personality development, cultural behavior and social and political status, and how they impact contemporary American racial relations. She also investigates aspects of the racial complex including archetypal shadow as core, constellations and their expression, and cultural trauma in the African diaspora. The book concludes with a discussion of racial complexes as a continuous psychological state and how to move towards personal, cultural and collective healing. Analyzing Jung's work with a renewed lens, and providing fresh comparisons to other literature and films, including *Get Out*, Brewster extends Jung's work to become more inclusive of culture and ethnicity, addressing issues which have been left previously unexamined in psychoanalytic thought.

Due to its interdisciplinary nature, this book will be of great importance to academics and students of Jungian and post-Jungian studies, sociology, politics, history of race, African American studies and African diaspora studies. As this book discusses Jung's complexes theory in a new light, it will be of immense interest to Jungian analysts and analytical psychologists in practice and in training.

Fanny Brewster is a Jungian analyst and Professor at Pacifica Graduate Institute, USA. She is the author of *African Americans and Jungian Psychology: Leaving the Shadows* and *Archetypal Grief* (both Routledge).

THE RACIAL COMPLEX

A Jungian Perspective on Culture and Race

Fanny Brewster

Routledge
Taylor & Francis Group

LONDON AND NEW YORK

First published 2020
by Routledge
2 Park Square, Milton Park, Abingdon, Oxon OX14 4RN

and by Routledge
52 Vanderbilt Avenue, New York, NY 10017

Routledge is an imprint of the Taylor & Francis Group, an informa business

British Library Cataloguing-in-Publication Data
A catalogue record for this book is available from the British Library

Library of Congress Cataloging-in-Publication Data
A catalog record has been requested for this book

ISBN: 978-0-367-17767-6 (hbk)
ISBN: 978-0-367-17770-6 (pbk)
ISBN: 978-0-429-05760-1 (ebk)

Typeset in Bembo
by Taylor & Francis Books

Dedicated to My Father and Forefathers

CONTENTS

ACKNOWLEDGEMENTS

I wish to thank the C.G. Jung Societies, Psychotherapy Institutes, the Salome Institute of Portland, Oregon, the C.G. Jung Institutes, Jolinda Osborne and Satya Doyle Byock. They welcomed me to be a part of their public and analytical training programs. They have generously opened their doors to me as we engaged in the material of this book. I appreciate their kind generosity that gave me the space and time to speak with them about this book as it was developing.

Thank you to Samuel Kimbles for his generosity of spirit in writing the foreword to my book and his pioneering work *Phantom Narratives: The Unseen Contributions of Culture to Psyche*.

The Jungian analysts who have contributed in deep support during the writing of this book include members of my home analytical affiliations: Philadelphia Association of Jungian Analysts, and the C.G. Jung Institute of Los Angeles. I thank them for all their caring support.

Thank you to Matthew Silverstein, at Antioch University/Los Angeles for his trust and spirit in being a believer in what we have shared in our community gatherings and his community's contribution to this book.

I wish to thank Pacifica Graduate Institute faculty and community members who were gracious in welcoming me into the Pacifica family as Core Faculty and by doing so provided me with the positive energy necessary to produce this book.

My gratitude to Sylvia Perera for all that she has generously given.

It has been a gift to have Christine Lewis and Sukey Fontalieu in my life as I do the work of being a writer. Thank you.

My appreciation to Andrew Samuels for his unwavering support.

Susannah Frearson my editor at Routledge Publishing has offered steadfast and valued guidance for which I am very grateful.

PREFACE

In *The Racial Complex: A Jungian Perspective on Culture and Race*, Dr. Fanny Brewster shares her reflections on how racial unconsciousness functions in Analytical Psychology, its literature, and its training programs. She introduces the Racial Complex and develops ideas regarding this complex through her use of Jung's concept of Complexes Theory. Using complex theory allows her to expand, deepen and open to our unavoidable racialized experiences in America in general, but more specifically in relationship to the silence and avoidance she noticed operating in the historical background of Analytical Psychology, its theories, and training programs. She says in her introduction, "I can say with certainty that Jung's minimalist idea of a racial complex was never discussed as any part of my analytical training, or anywhere within the Jungian community within my presence, except when I attempted to broach the subject in candidate training discussions of Jung's writings."

Through sharing of professional and personal experience as a Jungian analyst and a candidate, Dr. Brewster shines a light on racial dynamics that operate both in the background and in plain sight in our psychological theories and in our American collective culture in general. Using complex theory allows her to pull back the shades from our eyes, while allowing us to potentially see ourselves in context of these dynamic cultural forces through what she identifies as the Racial Complex.

Issues of institutional racism and social injustice covered over by privileges are discussed furthering our knowledge of the cultural features of a collective Racial Complex. Pairing the term Racial Complex with other Jungian concepts of the shadow, and archetypes, Dr. Brewster recognizes cultural trauma, cultural complexes and very importantly the potential for addressing cultural healing.

Sam Kimbles
author of
Phantom Narratives:
The Unseen Contributions of Culture to Psyche

1

INTRODUCTION

The Racial Complex: A Jungian Perspective on Culture and Race explores and re-envisions C.G. Jung's conceptualization of *The Theory of Complexes* in relationship to a black and white *racial complex* from an Africanist Jungian perspective. In the practice of Jungian psychology and American society, there has been much clinical and social recognition regarding parental complexes, the guilt complex, and various other complexes—even a Cinderella princess complex. Jung very briefly mentioned racial complexes in his essay, "The Complications of American Psychology" (1930):

> Just as the coloured man lives in your cities and even within your houses, so also he lives under your skin, subconsciously. Naturally it works both ways. Just as every Jew has a Christ complex, so every Negro has a white complex and every American a Negro complex. (*Collected Works*, vol. 10, para 963)

However, there has not been any Jungian literature specifically addressing this complex by name—*as* a racial complex, or by theoretical investigation, with two contemporary exceptions. These exceptions include Samuel Kimbles' group-oriented text entitled *Phantom Narratives: The Unseen Contributions of Culture to Psyche* (2014) with his extensive writing on the cultural complex and ethnicity and Michael Vannoy Adams who wrote the *Multicultural Imagination: Race in the Unconscious* (1996).

Michael Vannoy Adams produced a thoroughly investigative text on the treatment of ethnicity pertaining to Africanist people within Jung's writings, and selected theories of Jungian psychology. When Adam's book was first published, during the time of our training to become Jungian analysts, I remember approaching him and chastising him for having written a book similar to one I had envisioned writing. Michael was a few years senior to me in our program. Suddenly, he laughed and so did I. He probably laughed at my presumption to have even thought to write such a book. Maybe, he was just glad to have a discussion with me about his book and his own satisfaction at having written such a ground-breaking text at such a seemingly still-provincial time in our Jungian training institute—in the beginning of the 2000s. I am very appreciative of Michael's book—even more so now than back there in that beginning decade, when the word "race" was *still* only discussed at our training institute within the context of *The Collected Works*, and *only* as part of a theoretical model for Jung's collected unconscious. *Race* was a word and concept only permitted as a consideration in our discussions as written by Jung in his reference to Africanist people as "primitives" in *The Collected Works*. There was to be no classroom discussion of the inherent racial bias in Jung's writing, as expressed towards Africanist people in the formulation of his theory of the five stages of consciousness and intelligence hierarchy, with whites at the top and blacks at the bottom. There was no teaching in the analytical training program that attempted to deconstruct Jungian psychology, and make it inclusive in recognition of the ethnic diversity of our American collective.

As I think about what Jung defined as our "Negro" and "white complexes," I remember those years in training to become a Jungian analyst when I became "constellated"—emotionally disturbed, "triggered," aghast—in reading and discussing his point of view regarding Africans. In looking back, I realize with much greater clarity that there was absolutely no conversational place within the training environment to contest Jung's word, or to speak of my own discomfort at having Africanist people labeled savages and primitives. This is one reason why I now wish to engage with the racialized Jungian language and ideas of *The Collected Works* (Brewster, 2017).

How are we to decipher language that is painfully insulting and denigrating to selected cultures if we do not have open discussion regarding this type of language? The unspoken code of silence that dominated training in my Jungian training institute prevented such discussions. Helen Morgan, British Jungian analyst, says the following in her *British Journal of Psychotherapy* article, "*Issues of 'Race' in Psychoanalytical Psychotherapy: Whose Problem Is It Anyway?*" (2008).

> Whilst all sorts of differential power relationships prevail within any society which will inevitably reverberate throughout any of its institutions, I am focusing only on the matter of colour racism here. This is because of the curious fact that this difference is by definition so visible and yet we seem to be so blind to it. What might be thought of as a rather noisy problem has a particular sort of silence within so that we in psychoanalytic institutions seem unable to talk to ourselves about it. After all, we are rarely reluctant to talk and think about other matters that seem to be unspeakable, and we assume that harm is being done, not only to the part that is not being spoken about or to, but also to the one who is silent. My raising the question of what is it that we as white psychotherapists lose when we fail to talk about this matter is not merely a concern for a lack of richness in the cultural make-up of our institutions, but something more subtle, more damaging, a real emotional and intellectual impoverishment of the 'white' psyche. (pp 34–49)

Thinking back to those analytical training institute times I now also realize an aspect of this code of silence was its prohibitive nature against language or behaviors that activated almost any complex—it really didn't matter which complex was beginning to show itself or being constellated. All uncomfortable feelings and reactions were to be brought to one's analyst. They were never to be identified or acknowledged within the classroom training setting. At my institute there was no group processing experience except for an annual weekend retreat. Typically, during this retreat Shadow issues between the candidates emerged that had been contained by the structure of the institute's policy against open discussion during our weekly classroom and group supervision trainings. As a result of the three days' retreat time together, more unconscious material was activated but released to Shadow by our return to training the following Monday morning. There was just no place to "work-through" any of that intense psychological material with one's peers or analytical training teachers—who themselves had gone through the same analytical training program, usually at the same institute.

I can say with certainty that Jung's minimalist idea of a racial complex was never discussed as any part of my analytical training, or anywhere within the Jungian community within my presence, except when I attempted to broach the subject in classroom discussions of Jung's writings. I can also say there was no attempt to discredit or correct Jung's racial theories regarding Africanist people or his negative racialized language. I choose to write about Jung's Complexes Theory because it does allow for a re-visioning for our American collective in terms of race, racism and the accompanying psychological training and practice of psychoanalysis.

I hope it will also allow for an inclusion of a psychological idea—that of a racial complex, that inadvertently promotes racism by its very nature, finding its way into a general discussion in our American collective.

One of Jung's main tenets was that we must be willing to journey into the darkness—into the place where we are very uncomfortable and where we must ask the most difficult questions. I believe that as Americans we remain in that darkness and are still struggling to find ways to mediate all aspects of racism in our society. Societal discussions regarding racism especially between whites and blacks have been non-existent for decades with few exceptions of "cultural complex eruptions." Ignoring our deeply unconscious cultural racial problems and crises whether European, Middle Eastern or American has not made them go away.

Each chapter of *The Racial Complex: A Jungian Perspective on Culture and Race* presents differing views of the historically unexamined racial complex, and the polarization that exists in black/white psychological relations, as evidenced by American racism in selected areas of American life.

The Racial Complex explores Jung's Theory of Complexes and examines its components—including Jung's expressed ideas of American racial relations, which he indicated as part of the "complications of American psychology." In Chapter 1, "The nature of complexes," C.G. Jung's essay, "The Review of Complexes Theory" provides a frame on which to build narrative development of the concept of a racial complex. This chapter on complex theory mirrors, highlights, and deepens our understanding of how unconscious psychological processes such as complexes influence our ego consciousness thinking, and our collective human behavioral interactions.

Chapter 2, "The Racial Complex," introduces and expands on the concept of the racial complex as perceived from an Africanist point of view. Jung's reference to an American racial complex was minimal—four sentences, and never fully explored in his Collected Works.

Many complexes—Oedipal, parental complexes—have become major clinical markers in Jungian psychology. The absence of discussion regarding a racial complex reflects our reluctance to directly engage this complex on a collective level in our institutes—whether they are American psychological training institutes or institutions of higher education. This appears to be the most available place for discussions of racism within the field of education and what I have identified as the negative effects of a racial complex. The American racial complex is discussed in Chapter 2, "The racial complex," as an equally important complex, as compared with more familiar psychological complexes.

Chapter 3, Childhood: The shaping of psychological complexes," discusses childhood, parental and cultural engagements and the early life period when racial complexes can begin to be formed and shaped by environmental influences.

Chapter 4, titled "A cultural constellation," reviews and explores historical and social events that exemplified American moments of racial tensions and eruptions of the racial complex.

Chapter 5 of the book, "Archetype, Shadow, complex," considers the archetypal Shadow as central and core to the racial complex. This archetypal energy with its emotional constellation can result in individual and/or collective acts of aggression and hate, based on a lack of considering how a racial complex—same as the other complexes, takes "possession" and control of ego functioning. In an acknowledgement of Shadow and what possibly lies hidden in this archetypal darkness, we are usually confronted by that which we wish to avoid or of which we truly lack psychological knowledge. The chapter describes psychic complexes constellations and how these show themselves in both conscious and unconscious ways.

Chapter 6, "Culture and race," explores how our culture sets us apart as belonging and establishes kinship between and among family members. This chapter shows the connection amongst individuals that form a group and how racial complexes form us and are an intricate part of how we exist as Americans within our different ethnic cultures.

Chapter 7, "Cultural trauma and the racial complex," delineates the book narrative showing the dialogic tension between cultural trauma and cultural complexes. These markers of American black/white relations co-exist as an American paradox that for example has promoted active brands of racism—the Ku Klux Klan, for example.

The counterpoint for social justice has evolved as well and created political movements such as the Civil Rights Movement.

The Transference is a most important aspect of Jungian psychoanalytical clinical work. In Chapter 8, "Transference and countertransference," questions are developed pointing to the relationship between clinician and client that arise as a result of racial complexes being constellated in the transferential field. Relevant discussions include how ethnicity can become both an unconscious shadowed issue within the clinical setting while showing its presence through racism in the collective at large. What is the unspoken relating that develops when race is never mentioned and treated as color-blindness by either patient or therapist or both?

In Chapter 9, "Emergence from grievance to grief," the connection between the psychological suffering of grievance due to racial harm (racism) and group behaviors that develop in reaction to this suffering. The chapter reviews a creative/ political self that develops due to this racial grievance as shown within individuals such as poets of the Black Arts Movement.

Chapter 10, "American cinema: *Get Out*," recognizes American film as a historical screen for seeing into racial complexes and American racial relations. This chapter exams a critically and socially successful film, *Get Out*, that shows how film has captured the imagery and imagination of cultural white and black racial complexes.

Jung stated that we must be able to live with paradox and that this is an aspect of remaining 'sane' in an 'insane' world. Chapter 11, "The paradox of race and racism," proposes that racism is inherently paradoxical in several ways beginning with and including its demand that different ethnic groups "be" of different races when we are actually only one race. A discussion of the paradoxes of racism shows how psychologically difficult it is to live with racial complexes while understanding and living within a paradoxical American societal frame of racism.

In his writing of The Complexes Theory, Jung informs us that complexes are forever—we learn about them, adjust to them but they are ever present in our unconscious until they have become conscious through eruption. Chapter 12, entitled "Healing cultural and racial trauma," explores racial complexes as a continuous psychological state of which we can become more consciously aware. Through exploration we question how to move in the direction of personal, cultural and collective healing knowing that complexes never cease to exist in the unconscious.

It appears important to fill what seems conscious and/or unconscious gaps in post-Jungian 21st century literature, American Jungian clinical practice, psychoanalytical training program curriculum and the general American psychoanalytical/psychology field, regarding the racial complex and its connection to American racism. The notable absence, and perhaps avoidance of discussion of a racial complex within the field of American psychology, appears evident, especially today as we continuously find ourselves struggling to define and repair broken American racial relations.

Perhaps an exploration of Jung's Complexes Theory with a deepening perspective on the racial complex, and ensuing issues of American racism, will increase our individual psychological self-knowledge, as well as the collective understanding of those we consider our racial Other. The Racial Complex identifies the relationship between psychological issues of racism and historically uninvestigated racial complexes that can become constellated within and between Americans.

The unconscious process of the racial complex influences personality development, cultural behavior and social/political status—all aspects of the American collective. *The Racial Complex: A Jungian Perspective on Culture and Race* will hopefully further Jung's work in the area of complexes theory specific to black/white collective American psychology, cultural complexes, American racism and the Shadow archetype, in a way that promotes our cultural and racial healing.

2

THE NATURE OF COMPLEXES

The complex in psyche

We most commonly come to know and understand the complex because we develop specific behaviors or symptoms that give us psychological suffering. The clinical and relational work of being with unconscious material such as complexes would appear to require an understanding of how unconscious material such as complexes might emerge. I would like to begin by attempting to locate the abstract an elusive idea of psychological complexes before we enter into our first consideration of complex features and characteristics. This reminds me of doing dream work in which a classical stance is adopted by knowing the home of the dreamer's ego—where does the dream take place in terms of the dreamer's ego consciousness? In this case it is helpful to have a location in order to better understand what the unconscious dream material is attempting to tell us. This does require a connection with ego consciousness. The ego becomes a dream observer in service of later offering interpretation to understanding aspects of archetypal direction. This brings us into the heart of the unconscious where our dreams are created and can emerge into ego consciousness.

The unconscious psyche is that place within us that "contains" consciousness, the personal unconscious and the collective unconscious. The creativity of the unconscious or psyche is due to its ability to encompass us in keeping us balanced, like the earth in relationship to the moon and the sun.

We do not worry about losing our balance because gravity, like our ego, keeps us in place, giving us a conscious knowingness about our life in a basic way, even though it is not the sum total of who we are as human beings and not the central guiding center for all of life experiences. I think of the unconscious with its Self archetype as this place of centering consciousness that is beyond just ego consciousness. The integration of different events of consciousness to which I belong allows me to have a limited knowingness about both my human and divine nature.

In finding the home of the complex within psyche, we enter an understanding that such a place as psyche can exist. Jung says, "We must however, accustom ourselves to the thought that conscious and unconscious have no clear demarcation, the one beginning where the other leaves off. It is rather the case that the psyche is a conscious-unconscious whole" (*On the Nature of the Psyche, Collected Works* vol. 8, para 397).

In following Jung, we come to know that "something," psyche, holds us beyond the space of ego awareness. Many times we discover this place of otherness—other than the ego, because we begin to suffer emotionally or psychologically in a manner to which the ego is unfamiliar. This becomes a time when we search for that "other" place that may eventually lead us to a therapist or analyst who addresses our unconscious selves. Within this context we can learn psyche's language and elements and a perhaps unfamiliar path to psychological healing.

In one reference to the personal unconscious Jung says, "As to the no man's land which I have called the 'personal unconscious,' it is fairly easy to prove that its contents correspond exactly to our definition of the psychic" (*CW*, vol. 8, para 397).

He then asks the question: "But—as we define 'psychic'—is there a psychic unconscious that is not a 'fringe of consciousness' and not personal? This brings us to that place in psyche—the personal unconscious where it is believed that complexes reside, move and agitate."

In *The Structure of the Psyche* Jung offers this definition:

> The personal unconscious consists first of all those contents that become unconscious either because they lost their intensity and were forgotten or because consciousness was withdrawn from them (repression), and secondly of contents, some of them sense-impressions, which never had sufficient intensity to reach consciousness but have somehow entered the psyche. (*Collected Works*, vol. 8 para 321)

A second area of significance for locating complex material within the unconscious is within the shadow. As time passed, those practicing in the area of Jungian psychology developed an expansive language from Jung's original definition of shadow. However, it was Carl Jung who initially spoke of shadow as being an aspect of the personal unconscious. "the shadow ... represents first and foremost the personal unconscious, and its contents and therefore can be made conscious without too much difficulty" (*CW* 9ii, para 19). It would be considerably simpler to recognize how the shadow with all of its hidden unconscious desires, wishes and needs would have a place in the personal unconscious. Jung asks the question—isn't all of our individual material personal anyway?

A difference of importance between the personal unconscious and the collective unconscious is that the latter is based more on instinctive patterns of archetypal energies that we have inherited across generations.

We inherit these patterns as part of being human beings. We do not need to learn how to evoke the archetypal energy that flows through the collective unconscious. These energies exist as aspects of our consciousness without our will or control. In this way, they share the compulsive pull of the complex. Once we become aware of these types of energetic pulls caused by libido shifts in the unconscious, it takes consistent efforts and presence of mind to recognize the shifts. As with complexes, we are not dominating the energetic flow of archetypal energy. We become channels for this energy as we fall into amnesia and an ego blindness. We give over, only being able to view the loss of our ego-driven selves in hindsight, once the constellation of "possession" by archetypal and complex has passed.

Jung places the ego within a field of consciousness that makes itself aware through its own power of observation. We are born with ego and this continues through the span of a lifetime. Jung states that the ego is also a complex as well as sharing connections with other complexes. The ego's ability to live from the center of consciousness allows it to know many things about personality and daily aspects of survival. However, the ego is limited by its own consciousness. This is the field in which it dominates. When it enters the unconscious realm such as a dream state, it becomes less powerful. The ego's relationship with other complexes can be elusive. A major part of the ego's psychological work is defending itself against acquiring knowledge of its limitations. There is a need for it to believe that it knows everything or can know everything. The realization that it has limitations can cause great anxiety and distress. These limitations can be in any area of human life that is touched upon by ego.

The relationship between ego consciousness and complexes can become intensified when the former feels it is entering a place of unfamiliarity as is often the case when complexes become activated. The ego seeks to have the comfort of knowing where it is located in time and space. Complexes change the inner psychic landscape and usually trigger a shift in consciousness that is uncomfortable for the grounded ego. It is like the rumblings of an earthquake. Since complexes do not work in isolation, it is quite possible that two or more complexes will be activated at the same time thereby applying more pressure on the ego as it tries to defend itself against whatever the complexes are trying to reveal. When thinking of psyche as a system that is basically out of egoic control, it is possible that complexes that always carry emotions as an aspect of their psychic energy would have an even more frightening effect on the ego personality. This then is what causes stress on the psychological system of which psyche represents the entirety. Jung believed that the various parts of psyche work together in a coordinated way not only to keep the ego in balance—which is mostly knowing itself, discovering new things about itself, and maintaining comfort in that self-reflective place. Psyche's overall balance is maintained by laws of compensation between different states of consciousness. This becomes most significant in our individual lives when we cannot find the best way to live, behave or be grounded in our ego functioning ways.

The disruption caused to the ego can be thought of as a complex and archetypal problem of the Self that has gained libido power sufficient to interrupt ego complacency and processes.

A theoretical idea of classical Jungian psychology is that the Self archetype provides guidance even when it appears complexes are being activated that "antagonize" the ego. The elements of psyche that can be engaged at this time can appear to be behaving in a thoroughly undermining way for life but are actually moving within the unconscious and breaking across the threshold of ego consciousness in service of deeper psychological health. Complexes and the instinctive archetypal energy at their core interact with one another and may appear threatening to the ego and in ways they usually are because they signal incompatibility in the inner life and the need for transformative change in the outer life. This is generally not good news to the ego that seeks to hold its position within its own field of consciousness—demanding to continue in patterns of no-longer productive neurotic behaviors. The disruption of psychic life by complex constellation, archetypal possession/flooding or shadow work generally means that the inner psychic life is intensifying in a compensatory movement towards change in life patterns instigated by a Self archetype or Knowledge that is not readily available to ego consciousness.

Jung's Theory of Complexes

Jung gave the following definition of a *feeling-toned complex* in *A Review of the Complex Theory* published as a paper and given as a speech in May,1934.

> It is the *image* of a certain psychic situation that is strongly accentuated emotionally and is, more over, incompatible with the habit of consciousness. This image has a powerful inner coherence, it has its own wholeness and, in addition, a relatively high degree of autonomy, so that it is subject to the control of the conscious mind to only a limited extent, and therefore behaves like an animated foreign body in the sphere of consciousness. (*Collected Works*, vol. 8, para 201)

It was during the testing of research subjects on the Word Association Experiment from 1904 to 1910 that Jung noted the absence of a response to what he thought at first was a "failure" to the word test. Over some time the pattern that emerged to him was that particular words caused what he defined as "Gaps or falsifications of memory occur(ing) with average regularity in all spheres of association disturbed by complexes" (*CW* vol. 8, para 199). In other words, whenever one experiences the activation of a complex, there is a psychic, psychological and even physiological reaction that can be measured. The measurement is not only by length of time of such a delay in conscious response time but also to the emotional depth of the disruption to conscious, wake state clarity. The ability to remain focused diminishes. Jung says that he thanks Pierre Janet for being able to observe "the extreme dissociability of consciousness" (*CW* vol. 8, para 202) In this way, we learn from both Jung and Janet one of the major features of the complex once activated or constellated—that it causes one to become dissociated.

Jung in speaking of the difference between the academic professional and the psychopathologist relates how the former knows nothing about psyche in a way that is understood by the latter.

constellation = complex activation

fragmentation of psyche b/c of trauma.

that seems to be quite unknown to ... tion of dissociability of the psyche. ...connecting link between the psychic ...ne. Not only are unconscious pro- ... experiences of the conscious mind, ...nct loosening or discreteness. We all ... complexes and are to be observed ...xperiment. (*CW* vol. 8, para 365)

... issue of dissociation caused by the ...ing with his own question of "...

... go right over the threshold and become perceptible to the ego" (*CW* vol. 8, para 366). This would be in a more expectedly common, consistent fashion. The energy of what Jung calls a "subliminal secondary subject" would naturally seek to push out into our ego consciousness.

> This secondary consciousness represents a personality component which has not been separated from ego-consciousness by mere accident, but which owes its separation to definite causes ... the secondary subject consists essentially in a process that never entered into consciousness at all because no possibilities exist there of apperceiving it ... although, from the energy point of view, it is quite capable of becoming conscious. secondary subject does in fact have an effect upon ego-consciousness—indirectly or, as we say, "symbolically," though the expression is not a particularly happy one. The point is that the contents that appear in consciousness are at first *symptomatic*. (*CW* vol. 8, para 366)

It is important in defining the complex to understand how it affects our behavior—how we are changed usually without even knowing the extent to which we are different during the course of a complex activation or *constellation*. Jung's reference to the secondary personality component with its own libido energy source gathers this energy and becomes prepared to discharge this energy through a constellated effort. We experience and witness the results in the recognition of a complex behavior—through speech, bodily responses, thought patterns, shifts in ego awareness, any number of ways of knowing that we have been captured by a psychic dissociative moment known to us as a complex.

A second important feature of complexes is that the complex is itself created through fragmentation within the individual psyche. This fragmentation resulting in a complex is caused, Jung believed, by the experience of trauma. "The aetiology of their origin is frequently a so-called trauma, an emotional shock or some such thing, that splits off a bit of the psyche" (*CW* vol. 8, para 204). It is not difficult to imagine such an event happening to anyone of us when we consider that being born brings one into the possible realm of any psychological traumatic event once we leave our mother's womb. There is almost a guarantee of trauma beginning with the first "insult" of leaving the safety of the womb.

Childhood innocence is frequently disrupted by trauma—large and small situations that disrupt the ego's sense of safety. Very few of us enter the teenage years without some form of sadness or unhappiness marking the early growing up years. Sometimes it is the divorce of the parents, the death of a sibling, the substance abuse of a parent. These are major events but even the minor ones can cause us unhappiness due to the fragility of the young ego. Time spent in analysis is in most instances devoted to visiting and re-visiting moments in the childhood when traumatic situations occurred that at first might not even be recalled. Eventually, as the work continues and complexes are revealed, the relationship between the recalled memory and the suffering caused by that traumatized fragmented split off part of psyche are realized in what is usually an intensely emotional psychological experience.

Generally, we cry as we once again feel what the complex has almost demanded the ego forget because of a psychological anesthesia of amnesia. The inability of the developing ego to tolerate repeated trauma is supported by an unconscious forgetfulness that supports neurotic behaviors. The formulation of sequencing events all work to protect the mind, the inner psychological processes of us, and to later return us to a discovery of what we have lost due to early trauma. This then becomes the work of psychoanalysis. We use different kinds of language to describe how we enter this liminal space of psychotherapy. However, we know we have come because we have re-encountered something of our past that is unresolved. We can feel the slippage of a persona that has worked well for perhaps decades but is beginning to fail and many of us have no skills to deal with such personal "failures." The ways in which we have struggled to find internal states of peace away from neurotic suffering in the form of sadness, anxiety, dissociation or other emotional dis-ease fail to keep us safe. This is when upon entering psychoanalysis or psychotherapy the exploratory work of finding one's complexes begins, and continues long after therapy has "officially" come to an end.

We now come to a third characteristic of a complex. Due to the natural origin of complexes as an original aspect of our unconscious mental processes, we do not ever "lose" our complexes. They do have us not only in the moments of constellation but for a lifetime. Trauma, our neuroses, archetypal energies that flow from our individual consciousness belong to us. This is perhaps one of the most difficult elements of the complex to comprehend as the ego wants to feel itself able to divest of anything which is unpleasant to itself.

Complexes are not generally considered to be pleasant states of attention. When we are taken over by the emotions of our complexes we are generally re-visiting a moment of stress or as Jung has stated "duress." It is an unpleasant moment emotionally sometimes accompanied by shame or humiliation. Jung says the following regarding complexes:

> Complexes behave like Descartes' devils and seem to delight in playing impish tricks. They slip just the wrong word into one's mouth, they make one forget the name of the person one is about to introduce, they cause a tickle in the throat just when the softest passage is being played on the piano at a concert, they make the

tiptoeing latecomer trip over a chair with a resounding crash. They bid us congratulate the mourners at a burial instead of condoling with them, they are the instigators of all those maddening things. (*Collected Works* vol. 8, para 202)

In concluding he says, "As one might expect on theoretical grounds, these impish complexes are unteachable" (*CW* vol. 8 para 202). The fact of their unteachability leads us to gain a better understanding of how they might continue with one for a lifetime. I do however believe that we can learn to see into our complexes in a way that gives us insight and offers the possibility for change in our behaviors. This does not say our complexes are abnormal or should not be a part of our psychological development. We will have some psychological disruptions and emotional circumstances that will take hold of us along the way through childhood and into adulthood. We might call them complexes or by another name. In the tradition of Jungian psychology we call them complexes. These disruptions provide a way for us to consider ways of creating meaningful lives. Meaningful, according to my own bias, includes having not only material successes in life but finding one's way through a labyrinth of emotional and psychological challenges common to life. It means developing an understanding of the suffering that living entails and continuing in the struggle to engage with oneself on an ever-deepening level realizing that continuous daily psychological comfort is an impossibility for truly being human. Yet our humanity demands that we protect our selves. This protection, out of necessity, includes being fearful and having strong emotional defenses. These defenses include developing a strong enough ego structure to survive as adults. In his discussion of complexes, Jung says that the *via regia* of which Freud spoke, as the royal road of dreams was not actually true, Jung says that instead it is "the complex, which is the architect of dreams and of symptoms. Nor is this *via* so very 'royal,' either since the way pointed out by the complex is more like a rough and uncommonly devious footpath that often loses itself in the undergrowth and generally leads not into the heart of the unconscious but past it."

According to Jung, in our desire for protection, not just of our bodies but also of our ego consciousness—our sanity, we can be and are most often afraid of our own complexes. In further discussing this fear Jung states:

The conscious mind is invariably convinced that complexes are something unseemly and should therefore be eliminated somehow or other. Despite overwhelming evidence of all kind that complexes have always and are ubiquitous, people cannot bring themselves to regard them as normal phenomena of life. The fear of complexes is a rooted prejudice, for the superstitious fear of anything unfavourable has remained untouched by our vaunted enlightenment. This fear provokes violent resistance whenever complexes are examined, and considerable determination is needed to overcome it. (*CW* vol. 8, para 211)

We can fear our complexes and most times unconsciously wish to keep them hidden by shadow due to a feeling of shame about even having complexes—something that shows our limitations.

Complexes can be our secrets—hidden even from our own ego awareness. However, if psychological complexes are autonomous as Jung believed then we can exert some minimal control over them, once we become conscious of them, but we cannot always expect to avoid their emotional pull. In working with complexes within the clinical setting, there must first be a period of the clinician learning about complexes, and specifically about the personal complexes of the patient. The analyst will learn about her own complexes in relationship to the patient and the work that is being done and some point the complexes of family, culture and the collective in which the patient lives. Since the complex has fear as an aspect of itself, a part of the clinical work is allowing for this fear to be present in the transference, in the room. Typically, our egos do not wish to engage with anything that causes us fear. This is our nature. How do we permit the release of the energetic charge of a complex—which may arrive with or without the ego's permission, knowing it increases our fear and anxiety? This is also the clinical work of being with the complex—not always knowing how one will react and even what to do when we have foreknowledge. Psychic moments delivered by the unconscious are unpredictable by *its* nature and the ego must be prepared (this happens over time supported by ego strengthening), to discover and integrate new unconscious material as the clinical work progresses. This is a most valued element of doing psychological work—there does exist, I believe, a hope for transformation. This process of transformation might occur because of the recognition of complexes and our willingness to allow for them within the context of egoic growth and change.

An encounter with our complexes actually strengthens the ego in ways that it would never experience without the experience of engagement with its complexes.

Over time, as the clinical work continues we begin to learn that we are not only victims, hostages and gift-receivers of our complexes but they will bring us into contact with our family complexes. I believe that one of the most significant of these family complexes is that of the mother and father complex. Jung in writing about complexes appears to have written mostly regarding these two parental complexes. This writing is in *Collected Works* vol. 9i, "Psychological Aspects of the Mother Archetype" (1954/68). In this writing Jung expressed his belief in a positive mother complex as well as a negative one. The emphasis that Jung placed on the parental complexes suggests their importance as foundational base of all the complexes. Other Jungian analysts/writers who have followed Jung in this way include Hans Dieckmann who in *Complexes: Diagnosis and Therapy in Analytical Psychology*(1999) states:

> Hence, in my judgment, all the other complexes can be derived from these two great fundamental complexes, the mother complex and the father complex. This includes the brother and sister complexes in so far as brother or sister are more or less a rejuvenated edition of father or mother. We know from all analyses the extent to which the parental complexes play into the rivalries among siblings. In

her classic book, *Analysis of Children* (1930), Wickes elaborated for the first time the extent to which children live, suffer, and express the unconscious problems and complexes of their parents. (p. 3)

Our complexes therefore include psychic material that we have gained through early relationships with our immediate families. This broadens as we leave this family as children and move into the educational system as most children do after the first few years at home. It might be that whatever we have not obtained psychologically as parental complex "attachment" material via the family then grows through relationships with teachers, peers and others encountered in the more socialized environment away from the family. It appears that those first qualities of the developing complex fragment, perhaps caused by biological family issues or unresolved parental complexes issues passed via the intergenerational level, become the "image" of which Jung defined the complex. This image is not necessarily a direct picture of what exists in the childhood environment. The image may have the qualities and essence of circumstances that live in the childhood home.

The psyche, home to complexes, also has what Jung has referred to as *will* and *instinct*. In his discussion of these two possible activities in psyche, he says that human will cannot dominate that of which it knows nothing or very little—complexes. In a minimally instinctive manner, the complex behaves based on patterns influenced by an archetypal core or energies acquired and hidden in shadow. Following this, Jung provides a very comprehensive definition of the unconscious—that place of the unknown. He states:

> The unconscious is not simply the unknown, it is rather the *unknown psychic* ... the unconscious depicts an extremely fluid state of affairs: everything of which I know, but of which I am not at the moment thinking; everything perceived by my senses, but not noted by my conscious mind; everything which, involuntarily and without paying attention to it, I feel, think, remember, want, and do; all the future things that are taking shape in me and will sometime come to consciousness: all this is the content of the unconscious. (*Collected Works*, vol. 8, para 382)

I find beauty in this definition because it allows me to see Jung's wisdom in understanding our potential as human beings. When he speaks of himself as an empirical scientist, I might lose some of his intention. When he gives such as description as the one above I am aligned with him because of his expressive language in the definition. I understand that a part of this insistence was his proving of his research and the worthiness of Analytical Psychology as officially an area to be accepted and respected by colleagues and the public. However, when he provides the above definition of the unconscious—and he has given more than just this one, I see the broadness of his thinking as he projects onto the unconscious. It is like walking out of the house into the night and finding a darkened sky full of bright stars. It is noteworthy that when a complex moves into becoming activated we know it as being constellated—we become constellated, a human body that is charged with the energy of instinct and a force beyond our knowing until we come to recognize it through inner psychological work or self-reflection. We can think of ourselves as a field—a constellation of all that our complexes carry through both ego consciousness and archetypal energies.

3

THE RACIAL COMPLEX

Common complexes

In *The Structure and Dynamics of the Psyche*, Jung wrote the following in his description of the complexes:

> Today we can take it as moderately certain that complexes are in fact "splinter psyches." The aetiology of their origin is frequently a so-called trauma, an emotional shock or some such thing, that splits off a bit of the psyche. Certainly one of the commonest causes is a moral conflict, which ultimately derives from the apparent impossibility of affirming the whole of one's nature. (*Collected Works*, vol. 8, para 204)

We understand from Jung's definition of the complexes as just described that the complexes were originally a part of the psyche as a whole. Due to what Jung labels "so-called" trauma, we develop what eventually become complexes. It is important to note that he says the complexes are most likely caused by a moral conflict that keeps us from having a sense of wholeness. I think it brings together our understanding of how complexes—actual traumatized aspects of our psyche—reinforce a disconnection with the archetype of the Self. It is only through the conscious affirmative working of an alienated ego burdened with psychological complex issues that the aspect of psyche that seeks balance, through compensatory activity, can become more energized. I would call this, as Jung did, the archetype of the Self.

We come to know complexes as we have lived and studied these for almost one hundred or so years since first Wundt, Pierre Janet, Freud, and later Jung, helped us look into the unconscious, into psyche, seeking to better know ourselves.

Our attempts to understand our human nature leads us into that place not just of a Self archetype but also as Jung labeled it, the Shadow. (When used as an archetype reference then Shadow is capitalized, otherwise lowercase.) Today, as our understanding of Jungian psychology has grown, we also have a greater understanding of the Shadow as archetype functioning within us on an individual level as well as a collective level. I believe that our complexes hide behind and within Shadow and whatever archetypal core energy encompasses them until they choose to no longer remain hidden. Jung himself says:

> The complex can usually be suppressed with an effort of will, but not argued out of existence, and at the first suitable opportunity it reappears in all its original strength.

Jung says that the complexes play "impish tricks." These are some of the examples he provides in this essay of the *Collected Works* on the complexes in *A Review of the Complex Theory*.

As time has passed we have learned much more about our complexes in terms of labeling them and seeing how they might trap us.

This is true of particularly strong ones that can engage all of us at some point or another—for example, a guilt complex, a money complex, a sex complex.

Probably most known are the parental complexes, especially our mother complex. The emotional weight of our complexes tends to haunt us in our wake state as well as in our dreams.

Jung states that "unconsciousness helps the complex to assimilate even the ego" resulting in "a momentary and unconscious alteration of personality known as identification with the complex. He later says that this identification was spoken of as possession—being driven by the devil or "hag-ridden." This is more of the serious nature of the complex that we might encounter, and there is no attempt on my part of make little of our mother or father complexes—they bring us, and keep us in analysis, working on them for literally years.

The racial complex

I was first drawn to Jung's mention of what I have termed the *racial complex* through his comment in the *Collected Works*, in which he said the following:

> Just as the coloured man lives in your cities and even within your houses, so also he lives under your skin, subconsciously. Naturally it works both ways. Just as every Jew has a Christ complex, so every Negro has a white complex and every American (white) a Negro complex. (*Collected Works*, vol. 10, para 963)

At the time of these words Jung had begun writing about America's ethnic situation—what he believed were the problematic racial differences between whites and blacks and the cause(s) of such differences. Though he did not say very much in this particular paper, titled "The Complications of American Psychology" (1934), he emphasized the negative "fall-out" from the influence of the "primitive"— African and Native Americans—on white American society. It seemed important to expand on Jung's initial writing about the racial complex—Negro and American, because in referring to African Americans he only identified their desire to become white—to change ethnicity.

Embedded in Jung's minimalist comment is so very much that speaks to our unconscious processes of race and racism in America. As with much of Jung's work from decades ago, it rests with others who have an interest to deconstruct, refine and examine for applicability his theories to our 21st-century lives. I believe that within us and at times holding us are psychological complexes. I also believe that a complex that is devoted to raciality, racism and ethnicity does exist. At the time of Jung's bare reference to what I have termed a racial complex he could only identify an Africanist wish to be white and the white torture of African Americans living under the former's skin. His focus was initially on skin color differences as a determining factor for defining intellectual functioning, spiritual beliefs and interpersonal behaviors. I think that many of our American Jungian community have probably been uncomfortable with Jung's words from the 1930s, these words with their negative racial commentaries generally about African Americans and specifically about those of Africanist lineage. As a result, I believe that we have, like the larger collective, cultural racial complexes.

As an Africanist individual I do not have a white complex as Jung stated because I wish to be white. I have a cultural racial complex that embodies all that I have inherited due to this life—personal associations, the lives of my ancestors and archetypal patterns of all that has come before.

In discussing how Freud became the modern day discoverer of the unconscious, Jung addresses the issue of complexes. He says:

> The via regia to the unconscious, however is not the dream, as he thought, but the complex which is the architect of dreams and of symptoms. Nor is this via so very "royal," either, since the way pointed out by the complex is more like a rough and uncommonly devious footpath that often loses itself in the undergrowth and generally leads not into the heart of the unconscious but past it.

I can appreciate Jung's idea and image of the complex as a devious footpath because it suits one of my ideas regarding a racial complex. I would like to return to shadow for a moment—the place where we hide in the "undergrowth" all the things we cannot tolerate seeing, feeling, experiencing. I think our racial complexes also can live in that dark place of shadow. It can become that rough footpath that keeps us falling down and leading us astray. African Americans I believe have known more on a conscious level regarding this fact because of being at the negative symptomatic end of the racial complex. The also very complicated racial relationships in American society have been well documented while there is still so much more to tell. Within the last 150 years we have more intensely begun to open up Pandora's Box regarding ethnic issues and racism in America. Actually, today I believe we have more of a dialogue than ever before. But if we are to believe Jung, these conversations will not eliminate our racial complexes.

I agree with Jung. One important circumstance for this is that complexes, as psychic material from the unconscious, develop and have a free will of their own.

I think the only control we can exercise—through free will—on these autonomous split off parts of psychic material is first learning about them, and unveiling them further through shadow work—seeing into our cultural individual and group defenses and by engaging in ego strengthening in support of discovering places where we project our weaknesses onto an Other.

What exactly are our racial complexes? As an African American I have a white American complex—or so Jung believed. How does it haunt me? How am I hag-ridden?

When I was a child my grandmother used to talk about haunts or hags riding people, and the things one needed to do in order to not incur the wrath of haunts or spirits. She also used to speak about the healing remedy for getting rid of haunts. Let's say my racial complex with its white complex haunting me lives in my unconscious self—lower case /s/. How might I be uncomfortable in my own skin, certainly with my identity?

How does my ethnicity cause me a repetitive experience of the psychological trauma of identity tied to race as an individual as well as tied to an American group identity? Growing up African American means that there are racial lessons to be learned at a very early age. The lesson of skin color differences bring with them sociological and psychological wounds and trauma of racism. This is a fact of living in America.

It is a personal experience as well as a known part of our American societal history. It is certainly my own cultural collective group experience.

The suppression, repression and amnesia of racial complexes has contributed to the wounding of our American psyche in terms of how we have continued over centuries to inflict physical and psychological pain, because of a constructed idea regarding differences due to ethnicity.

Collective cultural trauma shows itself as having a cultural racial complex that has been formed and nurtured by first slavery, and down through decades the racist aspects of American life. Jung's idea of the theory of Opposites has done much in probably an unintended way to promote American racism. Samuel Kimbles has spoken eloquently regarding the racial issues inherent in groups that have their own cultural rituals and rites of passage. One of the landmark rites was the passage of Africans to the Americas as slaves. This event I believe remains a very uncomfortable discussion topic for many Americans even though we have not even began to see deeply into the psychological trauma still being experienced by the descendants of slaves. American slavery was a horrific event that lasted for centuries. Unfortunately, in our unconscious amnesia, we continue to live out our fears through racial complexes expressed many times through racist actions. Jung says, "Complexes are something so unpleasant that nobody in his right senses can be persuaded that the motive forces which maintain them could betoken anything good" (*CW* vol. 10, para 211). There is no wonder we have avoided within our area of Jungian psychology a depthful discussion of racial complexes.

Dissociation in the s/Self relationship

Identity is crucial to our psychological health and well-being. We understand that from the very beginning of our biological and I would say psychic lives, including the DNA of the archetypes, we need recognition in the form of identity. Due to the issue of racial relations in America, we are taught early on about ethnic differences. Jung pointed to something that was present in our shadowed collective unconscious that was, and continues to be, acted out through negative racial acts.

I believe that when we cannot recognize or see ourselves because of a complex taking over ego consciousness, then we are limited in developing a connection between our ego selves and the archetypal Self. This dissociation in the s/Self relationship, in the situation I am referencing, belongs to the traumatic event of slavery and all that has followed in terms of racial identity problems as part of a racial complex in America. We have seen the struggle to find the "right" identity for African Americans—within African Americans themselves as well as in the collective at large. First called black African, then colored, nigger emerged and has re-emerged, black—the negative one and the one of beauty of the 1960s—finally we have arrived at African American, again. Our American collective has struggled with finding its identity in terms of how we will, and must be treated, because of skin color differences, and all that goes along with the cultural meaning of such a circumstance. The psychological trauma of being Other has its impact on people of color. We can be Other but a part of our consciousness makes the Other—the white person, also an Other. One of the aspects of white privilege and its cultural white racial complex is that it perceives itself as the only thing that can confer qualities such as "otherness." In the case of African Americans, these qualities, both consciously and unconsciously in the shadow, would have us be "primitive" and not rational minded or reasonable human beings. We would be unintelligent and slow to learn. These beliefs come from racial complexes that have lived unexplored within shadow for many centuries since the arrival of slaves in the 1600s.

The cultural collective that is African American has as a group been bound, not just by the act of physically being bound for centuries, but also the psychological suffering of being individuals held within a racist societal structure. This structure has controlled and promoted through conscious habits the educational, financial and emotional deprivation of this cultural collective.

I believe that this external imposition of a negative racial construct has supported the deepening of a negative racial complex within individuals and in group psychic consciousness. Lynching and development of groups such as the Ku Klux Klan are examples of this type of a negative group consciousness—a cultural complex that erupts into American society. Jung has stated that complexes are split off parts of psychic material originally caused by trauma. I have considered a specific complex, that of the racial complex partly because it has not been discussed in any manner within historic Jungian psychology circles with the exception of Jung's reference to it in 1934 and American psychiatrist John Lind in 1909 with his publication of the article, in the first issue of the *Psychoanalytical Review*.

I would look to Jungian practitioners to open up a dialogue on one of Jung's theories emerging from his work on the Word Association Experiment. The racial complex is one such under-developed theory. I feel that it is left to us Jungians to begin these conversations. I have considered a written discussion of the racial complex because I believe we are caught in this complex, in a constant struggle with it, while attempting to forget about its existence. The pain of such a complex, as Jung noted, left us no peace. The very real suffering of racial discrimination and even physical death due to one's identity can cause severe emotional trauma. It can feel like the never-ending waves of a tsunami because thus far it has not come to an end. The days of mass lynching of African Americans have passed. However, the words alt-right, states rights, voter suppression and white nationalists all date back to a time when psychological and physical trauma were daily events for Africanist people. I believe the African American has not only the collective fear of such events held in an Africanist psyche but also the individual anxiety at the continuous possibility of being physically harmed due to skin color.

As I stated earlier I think there has been a reluctance to discuss a racial complex in our Jungian collective. Jung himself predicts that this could happen due to the very "devilish" nature of complexes—they only appear to be adequately suppressed by the ego only to come back stronger. Jung identified the Germanic group cultural complex that could be seen in the rise of Nazism leading to the Second World War. This rise of a group of people who participated in the murder of millions showed a distinct manner in which complexes can take hold of us. Individuals made up the armies, medical staff and administrators that formed Hitler's Nazi party. The victims of the trauma of this persecution were also individuals. Sometimes, I think we can lose sight of the importance of the individual—not just in terms of a process of individuation, which the Self promotes, but when dealing with complexes, as with the suffering that can occur. The numbers of those who have been tortured or murdered are so great that it is difficult to comprehend them and stay within our own ego's psychological place of comfort.

When complexes haunt us, we lack peace of mind. The trauma of racism and its effects does not disappear but accompanies one on a daily basis. I propose that any racial complex of African Americans will be closely "identified" with this type of trauma. I think it is important to stress what Jung knew: complexes do not disappear. They are uncovered. They are considered and worked with until we can learn how to live with them in some way that creates less continuous psychic and emotional pain. How can we do this—create less pain originally caused by an initial traumatic event such as the African Holocaust? I believe that we must first open ourselves to conversations about historical collective trauma and intergenerational psychic pain lived out in every day contemporary life. Silence will only harm us. The re-occurring trauma experienced as a racial complex moves in relationship with the self and the shadow. I propose that this relationship creates anxiety and a fear specific to the trauma that initially caused such a complex to develop and becomes repeatedly realized through the generations.

The tension and anticipatory anxiety caused by issues of racial identity, discrimination and fear of physical harm could only intensify psychic pain and a separation or dissonance with the Self. I would imagine that the psychological work to reconcile the s/Self would be complicated—as Jung said of American psychology when addressing the issue of ethnic differences in America. In the final paragraph of his essay on complexes Jung says that he has only given us the "essential features of the complex theory."

> He does not provide the solutions that are created by the complexes but does say, "Three important problems would have to be dealt with: the therapeutic, the philosophical, and the moral. All three still await discussion." (*CW* vol. 8, para 219)

I believe that my discussion of an African American cultural racial complex, brought about by the trauma of the African Holocaust, and racism, is one avenue for looking at our deeply complicated American collective as well as individual problems in all three of these areas that Jung have posited—the therapeutic, the philosophical and the moral.

Complexes do not go away. We bring them into consciousness out of the shadow. We make the unconscious conscious. In the further comprehension of Jungian theories and concepts it is incumbent upon us to explore, discuss and examine those things that continue to haunt us. This the true work of being aligned with depth psychological work. I believe myself and others like me follow in a depth psychological way when we pick up the slender threads of the beautifully woven tapestry of consciousness and begin to create a different pattern with a familiar fabric. I think about the development of ideas regarding cultural racial complexes as being in alignment with this proposition.

Two aspects of racial complexes, exposed through racism, are emotional suffering and the pain of invisibility. These aspects combined with the struggle for identity are only a part of what I consider needs healing within the parameters of negative racial complexes. I can recognize these aspects because I have seen them played out in my own life, my family and my cultural collective. I have seen the results of negative racial complexes exhibited in the broader collective.

How do we begin to think about healing these places of psychic pain—of long standing psychological suffering? Most of us wish for and strongly desire a state of inner peace, a harmonic connection between our ego and our unconscious, in this case our archetypal Self. But Jung gives us almost a warning as regards our complexes as we seek harmony.

I think the beauty of Analytical Psychology is that it can oftentimes provide the answer to our suffering. The remedy is in the poison. I believe that Jungian psychology is a psychology of discovery. The path will usually be in the form of a labyrinth—it will of course *not* be easy. The acceptance of this fact and the actual experience of both the suffering and joy of life—both the pain of the complex, and the numinosity of the divine Self, *can* continue to offer us hope.

In community

An aspect of my more recent Jungian-oriented work has been its expansion into speaking and facilitating group processes regarding racial relations for group dream work, Jungian clinical analytical training and community of individuals broadly interested in Jungian psychology and its practice. At a recent gathering at Antioch University, Los Angeles, a group of individuals—alumnae, students, faculty, Jungian analysts and community members met on a Sunday. We met in order to deepen our experience of one another within a multi-ethnic community of mostly strangers who were willing to think and feel through raciality, American depth psychology, racism and the racial complex.

Through the hours of being together we learned about our own biases—our individual racial complexes, our inner cultural hurting places and how to gain more courage in asking questions about our Jungian community, depth psychology, and racial issues. We began with the question I have asked in the second section of this chapter: what is a racial complex? It is not too simple of a question to return to here as I wish to bring in the voices of community.

Jungian psychology is known for its mostly structured format of a one to one interaction in the clinical practice. I believe that the Jungian material we seek to expand upon in terms of the racial complex suggests a gathering of many who are willing to enter a collective space. One of the difficulties with the racial complex and its archetypal shadowed material is its staying hidden. Jungian community gatherings and discussions, supports adding a format in service of deepening our conversations, on a topic that has hidden from consciousness for a very long while in American Jungian psychology. When we gather I will typically hear that those attending are eager to find answers and raise questions in a circle of others where vulnerability is allowed and no topic is forbidden. This definitely would be a Jungian circle coming together to discuss racial issues.

Within our group that day in response to the questions: What is a racial complex? What does this question mean to you as an individual? Some of the following participant responses were offered:

Paradox
On-going trauma
Skin color
3rd Culture
Historical trauma
Who am I
Self-Vanishing
Am I deserving?
Shame
Projections
Emotions
"Reading" the Other's signals
Vulnerability
Owning feelings
Suppressed humanity
"Sloppy" work

The openness with which we worked together in our group process reflects the difference in how we have been able unable to communicate about racial relations within our Jungian community. A part of the reason for *The Racial Complex* book is to further open our discussions within and without the area of Jungian psychology.

Group process allows us to share a part of our conscious selves as well as unconscious material—complexes, in a way that does not make us fearful to speak of shame, of ourselves or of others. As our group delved into the question of the nature of the racial complex we can see from the shortened list above that skin color, emotions, trauma and identity are each recognized as a part of this complex. Group participants related their own individual experiences with the "normal" of being a particular skin color—whether white, black or yellow, and the painful emotional encounters with others who find their skin color offensive.

The racial complex like any complex carries emotions. Jung named the complex as being emotion-toned for the reason of its carrying within it emotionality. This emotionality as previously discussed is not only fear due to ego consciousness—a loss of control over complex domination—but also the ego's fear of what this selected complex carries for the person of color. Regarding the emotions would be fear of death—African Americans have been killed in one form or another because of their skin color over hundreds of year. So within the anxiety of a racial complex for a black person is the ego's fear of a literal dying. Skin color and emotions are very much tied together as aspects of an African American racial complex.

The identity of black skin, brown skin, yellow skin signifying "Other," has carried its racial discrimination and resultant penalties for centuries.

Since complexes do not go away in our psyches, can endure for a lifetime—perhaps because of archetypal energies inter-generationally over many lifetimes, it seems very possible that the racial complex of a person of color is bound by the emotion of fear.

This fear has been solidified over generations by lynching, Jim Crow acts of violence and sexual assault against black women. In looking at the common complex and the ways in which it functions, how do we amplify its attributes in terms of the racial complex? For example, in considering how a complex is as Jung says "unteachable," how do we imagine this would be actualized in a racial complex? Is there a way in which we can "teach" ourselves to behave in a non-racist manner towards someone that we "hate" because of skin color? Can we "teach" our racial complex to "behave" in the face of our own fear of ourselves and of another? How do we teach ourselves not to be afraid when physical violence and death is such a real possibility because of skin color?

I believe that suppressed humanity and shame as highlighted by group members and therefore within this book's discussion belong together. They can also be discussed as separate affects but cohesions of the racial complex. How do we define shame? What is suppressed humanity? As I listened to a young woman speak of what it felt like to be black, to have "a suppressed humanity," in that moment it was as if I could feel her "disappear." Someone from the above list spoke referencing the question of her racial complex in terms of self-vanishing. I could see in those moments of our discussion and feel within the phenomenological space the quality of making one's self disappear due to shame and the suppression of self that merged together in a number of complexes driven by an autonomous cultural racial complex. Complexes are not singular entities and as elements of the psyche do not exist by themselves without influence by other psychic energies in the unconscious. A multiplicity of them may and will generally interact with each other at any time that one may be constellated. In speaking of complexes Jung says the following regarding shame:

> It is not immediately apparent that fear could be the motive which prompts consciousness to explain complexes as its own activity. Complexes appear to be such trivial things, such ridiculous "nothings," in fact, that we are positively ashamed of them and do everything possible to conceal them. (*Collected Works* vol. 8, para 207)

The irony of shame becoming activated in the psyche of an African American individual tied to a racial complex is informative and yet not surprising. Racism demands that within the ethnically different relationship, one individual must overtly carry shame. All of the lessons of American racism dating back to slavery adhere to the rule that people of color much be the carriers of shame. This is a harsh irony. When viewed within the context of a white/black racial complex, who has more to be ashamed of on a cultural level?

When we consider shame within the psyche of an African American woman or man can we think about "deserving"—also from the above list? An emotional positioning within the psychology of having the intergenerational trauma of the affects of slavery addresses worthiness and deserving of the best—deserving of anything. The tradition of slavery and the years following speak to giving the worst—the cast offs, to people of color. How does shame hide in the psychic space of shadow for all these hundreds of years? When a racial complex is triggered by a sense of worthlessness that appears in behaviors or feelings of shame and being undeserving of good, can we not help but see patterns of self-destruction.

Who speaks for our worth and how do we better learn the inner language of self-value?

These were questions raised at our Sunday gathering in our discussion of the racial complex. The racial complex within African Americans promotes a sense of polarity. This polarity is reflected in the American cultural collective in all-American ethnic groups. We have discovered the falsity of declaring us as being a Melting Pot. We are not that but rather more like Jambalaya. We arrived to America in different ways and have survived within our cultural groups through adversity—some of us more than others. I believe that we have learned to live out Jung's theory of Opposites in a sociological as well as psychological manner through our racial complexes. The polarity that was spoken of by the woman participant was addressing not only her inner sense of being segregated from within—being split off from the Self perhaps— but feeling alienated in a home, town, school to which she felt she should belong. She feels a polarity because her racial complex when activated connects with a sense of isolation and rejection by an Other that refuses to accept *her* cultural differences. In the world of Opposites and polarity, there can only be one "Other" that is acceptable. History, cultural emotional pain, collective racism have all defined for the African American individual experiencing a negative racial complex constellation, which Other is acceptable. This decision as repeatedly experienced, like the endurance of any complex, lives in the racial complex.

In our Sunday discussion, different voices kept returning to the word *trauma*. We also spoke of historical trauma. These are words that continue to return into our daily conversations not only in the room that day at Antioch University, but also in the media, our family rooms and our social settings. We can't seem able to stop speaking of our trauma. I feel that as people of color it took us so very long to arrive at this destination in this time when we can almost touch, not yet fully embrace our historical trauma. It sometimes still hurts too much as an individual and as someone belonging to the culture of ancestral slavery. The centuries that we were born into and lived in human bondage are a part of our historical, inter-generational trauma. We have barely begun to feel ourselves and hear our own voices awakening to this trauma. It does not appear that we are ready or prepared to relinquish this historical trauma. This history and all the historical lies told and truths omitted in American history have added to an American collective racial complex that also exists within each of us who have experienced living on American soil even those who have arrived as immigrants—white, brown, or yellow. In America there are "racial rules" for every "colored" body.

African American historical trauma includes the African Holocaust. We are not forgetting because we are only now waking up to another consciousness of remembering. This history of ours, that includes such a fierce hypocritical denial by the racist structure of American society, has supported and encouraged the development of a racial complex that though I am only discussing here with a focus on whites, actually belongs to all Americans. Jung's perspective on the racial complex in terms of whites was that the "negro" under the skin of whites.

This image of African Americans as irritant has persisted through the centuries with Africanist people as "the problem." This denial of us as worthy, a part of humanity, deserving of a non-enslaved life, has become a sometimes repressed, sometimes active part of American consciousness. I believe it is a part of why we struggle with racism and display all the symptoms of racism through our attitudes and behaviors. In the collective there has been centuries-long denial of racism and racist actions all flour-ishing underneath white privilege. In the burying of Africanist people needs, wellness, prosperity, the repression of their goodness, what arises in the unconscious actions of a white Other signals the presence of trauma in the form of a racial complex in the personal unconscious.

The historical trauma of the African Holocaust I believe resonates so much more loudly now than ever before in our awakened consciousness because we have had so many centuries of denial regarding its existence. The stories and narratives of slavery were not considered important in telling the history of the Americas. The cursory telling of the lives of millions who died in the Middle Passage and as part of North

American slavery created a quilt of comfort under which American collective tragedy could reside in shadow.

What about white guilt?

This was part of a question posed by a group member. I would ask what about a white guilt complex in duality with a white racial complex? How do these complexes present themselves in terms of race, racism, behaviors and attitudes?

Another woman addressed her own personal issue of not believing that she could own anything—that nothing could ever really belong to her—ever, not even her own feelings. She was afraid everything could be taken away from her. She believes this is a part of her racial complex as a black woman. The first response to her came from a white man. He said that he doesn't think about such a thing, ever—because he was raised as a white American male to think of ownership of *anything* as a natural way of functioning.

Is this a part of white privilege—part of a cultural white racial complex? What do centuries of slavery and ownership of millions—human beings, land, money—do to the complexes and collective unconscious patterns of psyche that reflect ethnicity?

I view the Sunday that we spent together at Antioch University as a continuation of Jung's work on complex theory. I don't think that we can have only one location—solitary rooms for all the questions, concerns and rhythms of psyche that present in our individual experiences or within our 21st-century collective. I do believe that we must occupy every space that we can with inner and outer conversations because the tenacity of our racial complexes are relentless in their ability to survive, remain strong, and cause emotional pain.

In *The Complications of American Psychology* Jung states the following:

> Racial infection is a most serious mental and moral problem where the primitive outnumbers the white man. America has this problem only in a relative degree, because the whites far outnumber the coloured. Apparently he can assimilate the primitive influence with little risk to himself. What would happen if there were a considerable increase in the coloured population is another matter. (*CW* vol. 10, para 966)

Perhaps the *racial infection* to which Jung refers is actually our racial complexes. We as Americans have certainly *all* been infected no matter the size of population.

Apparently, one of the most relevant fears of some who have a cultural white racial complex, one hundred years after Jung wrote the above words, was that the colored population *is* increasing. What would happen if there was a considerable increase in the *colored*, black and brown population?

4

CHILDHOOD: THE SHAPING OF PSYCHOLOGICAL COMPLEXES

Early trauma

The early beginnings of trauma shape us more then we can know or remember.

My first world of color consisted of brown pecans with streaks of black that had fallen into my gardener-grandfather's yard. This first world included persimmon fruit hanging on trees and concord grapes lazing across an arbor. My first identification as a brown child grew seamlessly into and out of my consciousness. My first world was full of brown people—my parents, my grandmother, my grandfather, aunts and uncles. All shades of rich chocolate. My friends at school and my Catholic nuns, my first teachers where I began Kindergarten and remained for eight years—were all chocolate-colored. My world of colors did not mean I was color-blinded. It only meant that I was born into a small southern town where segregation was a way of life. Even my pediatrician was my color—an unusual event in those days of strict segregation.

When I first noticed that my color meant something to anyone other than me or those in my immediate family it was because I started growing up and making occasional trips to downtown—across town, to where shop owners were white, water fountains were marked "colored" and the local movie theatre said I had to sit upstairs in the balcony. Though my parents spoke of racism and segregation and the Klan, my orientation to my world was that of being and belonging to a close, intimate group of individuals that shared my language, my food and religious traditions of the AME Church.

I attended the Catholic Church as I did the school but God was segregated, and the white priest was only a one-dimensional small part of my childhood world of colors. The disruption that came to my idyllic world of sweetness happened because I grew up.

Cornelius Eady says it very well in his poem "Buckwheat's Lament." A line there that says: *Wait 'til you're grown*. There is so much truth in those words. My childhood had a remarkable amount of innocence. This was largely because even when I was being hurt by a classmate, or someone else who had intruded inappropriately in my world, I didn't know how to take it as abuse or an insult. But I did not escape all of the turmoil in my childhood home—I think I had already begun to be numb from it at an early age. However, ego complex development in an otherwise rich cultural environment protected me from what might have later become severe acts of self-destruction.

Children demonstrate age-related developmental progression of race conception beginning with knowledge of color categories and culminating with conceptual awareness of racial categories. Children 3–4 years old for example are able to categorize by racial group based on color (brown or pink skin color), and 5–6-year-olds are capable of accurately identifying racial labels based on socially constructed skin color identifiers (black or white).

The shaping of racial complexes in children

We experience the introduction and growth of an ego complex that learns defense and self-protection.

I am proposing that in addition we also experience the development of a racial complex that shows itself through behaviors and racially related actions that can be of defense or aggression. This is not unlike what Jung was saying in the 1930s; he just didn't say very much about the racial complex. As I expand this theme of a racial complex I ask questions of myself that I wish to be shared. My first question: if the complex—in the case of the racial complex, is a split off part of psyche that comes from trauma, what might this trauma be for a black child? I think my first experiences of trauma as well as racial cultural awareness came through my parents. I also believe that my parental complexes—especially my mother complex—were an integral part of my initiation into the awareness of raciality. It was with my mother or grandmother that I generally traveled as a child in our small southern town. It was my mother who first forbade me to drink from a water fountain that had the words *Colored Only* written above it. It was my parents who sat speaking about "crazy" white men in white hoods who were terrorizing black people on Myrtle Beach. This was during the late 1950s and early 1960s. It was my mother who became infuriated with my grandmother when she sent me out to work picking cotton as a child one summer. This actually happened. I must have been 10 years old and was staying with my grandmother when my mother went to work.

My mother's fury was fire because she had a different vision for me—it included getting an education. These were the words spoken—getting an education. These were sacred words to a woman whose own mother had died at age 12 and who had to become dependent on family for every meal that she consumed. It meant the world to her that this would not happen to me and that I would get an education. My paternal grandmother's actions were in direct contradiction to what my mother dreamt for me. I have only seen my mother enraged four times in my life. This was one of those times. My mother was like a possessed person. I know now that an archetypal energy of rage possessed her. She could not and would not be persuaded from her wrathful rage and when it had passed through her she walked away from my grandmother without apology.

The trauma of a black child is unexpectedly getting up in the morning before dawn and going to a field to pick cotton all day with strangers. This is what had happened to my ancestors—to my great-grandmother. My grandmother herself must have done the same because she thought nothing about sending me to the fields. This memory of going to the fields was I believe an archetypal memory that still lived in the unconscious and became alive in my grandmother's behavior. My trauma that evening became a separated part of my psyche. My ego was shaken by the intensity of my mother's voice and her behavior towards her mother-in-law. A woman she had known for a quarter of a century. I witnessed rage in its purest form and it shook me to my core—to that psychological place where complexes are developed. I believe that day I saw the constellation of my own mother's parental complex as well as the archetypal energy of a mother archetype protecting her daughter and the emergence from a cultural shadow archetype that was dark and deep in my southern culture. I was traumatized.

I believe it is traumatizing for black children to observe the level of violence today that they can be exposed to not only on television but in their families and sometimes in their neighborhoods. I also believe that the effects of slavery on our ability as a cultural group to integrate and heal from the effects of this archetypal effect of slavery and Jim Crow has not disappeared. Our current life informs us that the effects of our cultural differences based on ethnicity have only gotten stronger in the daily political climate. African American children get shot and harmed because of many social factors. I would suggest that one of the hardest factors for our American collective to accept is that we as a collective are still traumatized from the effects of slavery. As Americans we can't put it to rest and because we cannot—African American children and their parents live under the gun. This is figuratively and literally. Poverty, a lack of education and the inability to shift ways of thinking keep us bound in a continuous cycle of seeing our children taken away through death or foster care. The trauma of the parent is witnessed, lived and re-lived within children of my cultural group. The individuals who are to protect and take care of these children can oftentimes commit violent acts against the African American children. There is a trend, a way of thinking amongst some whites that believe they are always at risk to be harmed by African Americans. As a cultural group, we most often think the opposite. For whites this shows up not only in believing that someone of color is going to snatch your purse but in so many other ways. For example—a white woman who calls the police on a man she sees running into a building. She calls the police and says that the man is "agitated." When the police come and find the man in the University of Massachusetts building they discover that he has been coming to that building to begin his day, as an employee for 14 years after his morning run. I can give you example after example.

A black woman in Brooklyn was standing out of the rain under the awning of a building waiting for her Uber to come. A woman tenant came outside of the building and told her to move or she was calling the police. This waiting black woman said I'm just waiting for the car service, I will move soon. It wasn't soon enough for the white woman. She then threatened the Uber driver with calling the police because he was picking up the Black woman who had long since moved into the rain from under her front door awning—onto the sidewalk. The entire situation was videotaped. The threat of the police is real. There is no mistake about that when you are a person of color—even a law abiding citizen.

When you are a person of color—the perception of wrongdoing on your part is increased 100 percent. How traumatizing is it as a child to grow up knowing that your mother is completely stressed and worried for your very existence? And that you may have a target on your back if you don't "act right"? Unfortunately, you have a target on your back no matter how you act. One last example—a tragedy. A man is in his apartment. A woman police officer enters his apartment. She lives in the same apartment complex. She shoots him claiming that she thought he was a criminal, was going to attack her. It is *his* apartment that she now claims to have entered in error but he is dead. She is white and he is a young black man.

Black children with their own constellated racial complexes will inherit anxiety and fear triggered by their complexes. Each complex has an emotional tone. Could I say that racial complexes can likely be activated with a tone of anxiety as well as anger? It is itself tricky to speak of anger as an aspect of a racial complex for African Americans.

This is because one of the most difficult projections to bear in the African American cultural has been that of "angry black people." This is because the cultural group deserves their anger. What is expected after centuries of slavery and centuries of collective denial?

Does anger belong anymore to a black child than a white child? Is it all projection onto that black child? Is that black child's own racial complex constellated by the emotions of his or her parents, a school teacher, a coach as influencing racial factor? I ask these questions because if I am to believe in the concept of the complex and that there does exist a racial one as Jung indicated, then should I not ask further questions than Jung related to the nature of this complex?

In the shaping of a black child's racial complex how much intensity and psychological suffering occurs because of collective institutional racism?

Joy DeGruy in her book *Post Traumatic Slave Syndrome* says the following:

> Slavery was an inherently angry and violent process … It's no wonder we're angry. Even when we're feeling good, an ever-present anger resides just below our surface. Anger at the violence, degradation and humiliation visited upon ourselves, our ancestors and our children; anger at being relegated to the margins of the society in which we live, anger at the misrepresentation and trivialization of our history and culture, and finally, anger at living in the wealthiest nation in the world and not having equal opportunity access to its riches. (p. 133)

We are at least at the point in our American collective where we can acknowledge that most American institutions included racism as a factor of their origins. It appears to me that the educational environment is a place that has oftentimes promoted the re-traumatizing effects of racial prejudice.

This would be from Brown v. the Board of Education in 1954 until present times. Most black children attend public schools. Many schools in black neighborhoods continue to be without sufficient books, optimal learning opportunities and sometimes even good drinking water—e.g. Flint Michigan—still. When we consider black children in mediocre learning environments with conditions that are this way, do we consider that racial prejudice is a part of the reason for such conditions and that these conditions help to shape a racial complex tied to complexes of low self-esteem or inferiority?

Black children exposed to racial prejudice whether it is in the poor conditions of the school or that of the teacher experience a reinforcing and constant re-exposure to the trauma of low self-esteem. The attempt to achieve is lowered by the low standards of expectation. The black child is expected to learn the elements of white culture—there was once a major ongoing confrontation as regards Ebonics. The black child must bear the pressure of forgetting his own cultural self in service of a white learning experience that mirrors very little of his family life or cultural group.

I can see the anxiety that would be a part of any black child's early educational learning experience. And it doesn't stop there. I have seen the insecurity of African American men and women in college who continue to manifest what shows up as inferiority complexes interacting and initially stimulated by a racial complex. The constant comparison of the knowledge possessed by whites and the fear of the lack of knowledge experienced by African Americans in a learning environment begins at an early age.

In remembering one of the features of the complex—it does not go away or disappear, I can see and hear stories from black adults who learned early on that they could not compete against white children and white "knowledge." The trauma of feeling inadequate and unable to learn and grow can lead eventually to dropping out of school. We see this in the attrition numbers of African American college students. How much does the re-traumatizing of a racial complex influence a lack of trust, confidence and focus on success in attaining a college degree for black students? I believe this is an important question. They ask themselves—am I the problem? The one with the problem?

The following quote is from the *Handbook of African American Psychology*:

> African Americans may demonstrate a unique experience of anxiety that is yet to be articulated in diagnostic texts. Studies show that panic disorder characterized by recurrent unexpected panic attacks, persistent concern about having another attack, and the implications and consequences of the panic attacks is uniquely presented among African Americans. (p. 402)

Complexes in themselves are not abnormal. They are aspects of the psyche that I would say have their own personalities. The results of the actions that come from the constellation of the complex can be viewed as negative or positive depending on the circumstance. Jung in speaking of the complexes said that whites had an experience of a Negro complex—under their skin, implying a negative experience. The Negro on the other hand Jung suggested wanted to be white. This is not a new way of thinking.

In our American collective we have had many discussions about how black people want to be white and vice versa—especially when Eminem began making his music. What is the trauma of envy and jealousy that can shape the child's ego?

Is it the negative of a cultural black racial complex to want better housing, the best education for one's self and children, a great job? Does the racial complex that develops in black children see the rich material life of a white Other and want to destroy it? I believe this question is operative even now in our collective. I believe that a part of what drives the energy behind the Trump movement is a desire to destroy what African Americans have accomplished since slavery such as affirmative action, civil rights, better opportunities for education. The possibility of Central Americans and South Americans coming here and also making achievements appear intolerable to many who want to "make America great again." What of the trauma caused to thousands of brown children brought here for a better life, separated from their parents and put into cages? What do we think about the traumatized racial complexes of *these* children? Many of whom are still separated from their parents as I write these words.

If complexes are "normal" then what is different about a racial complex? What can be good about it? I do believe that the recognition of the complex—like any other complex increases our awareness. Jung says that this is oftentimes all that we can hope for—increased conscious awareness. But is this *good enough* in the face of constellated racial complexes with heightened emotional tones of rage and anger? Is it the nature of this particular complex to always include racism, hateful acts and violence? I propose that the center archetype of this racial complex is Shadow. How does this play out in the lives of African American children already with a sense of powerlessness as most children have anyway?

Does racial prejudice instigate the development of this complex and its shaping in the direction of the negative? Is it "normal" to develop within my childhood mind and emotional body self-hatred because of my skin color? Does the trauma of the racial complex add to my defense in a collective that says I must be defended because safety can be sparse and I am always at risk. Not only because a larger collective says so, but also because it is a marked feature of my cultural collective. And besides that my mother and father have also told me so in support of my survival.

Is there normality to the racial complex? How does it show itself? I think there is because I want to deepen my self-understanding and the presence of this complex in my personal unconscious can create emotional pain and ego awareness. My experience of jealousy brought me to a deeper psychological place. In speaking with a white friend she began to cry with acknowledging that her ancestors had made their multi-million fortunes on the backs of mine through slavery. Later, I realized that a major emotion that came to me was one of jealousy—for what my ancestors had failed to achieve and what became a financial aspect of my life and that of my own ancestors. Before then I do not believe that I had a feeling, a sense of true jealousy. This emotion came directly as a result of my racial complex becoming constellated. I now knew what jealousy was and also what it was not in my own individual experience. If my people had been given reparations would I have experienced this emotion? I don't know—but it might have been met with just anger—a re-visiting of that emotional place rather than jealousy.

Hans Dieckmann in *Complexes: Diagnosis and Therapy in Analytical Psychology says*:

> In the healthy psyche, an entire system of different complexes, each with its unique quality, are related to one another. Through a partial identification, the healthy ego can make use of them when necessitated by various life situations to master the task at hand.

I do not pretend to have answers to all the questions I pose regarding the racial complex, racial prejudice and racism. I invite us to think over some of the ideas presented in this writing. Let us think about our own experiences as Americans, as Jungians and let us see what parts of Shadow the light can catch.

African American children and racial prejudice

I come from an ancestral lineage where racial prejudice was pronounced, destructive and pervasive in all areas of life. This is not a specific complaint. It is a fact of Africanist life. I need look no further than my own parent's lack of formal education and their insistence that I receive a good education to know this fact. The racial prejudice that my parents experienced was preceded by that of their parents, and their parents before them. I did not come from a line of slaves that made their way through the Underground Railway escaping north. My ancestors arrived in Charleston, S.C. on slave ships and remained in their Gullah community for centuries. The racial prejudice that greeted them also survived for centuries. When Dylan Roof went into a Charleston, South Carolina church and killed nine African Americans, I grieved not only for their lives but also for the members of my ancestral lineage who had to endure racial prejudice in that city as they stood on auction blocks and later worked the low country rice plantations.

Racial prejudice still exists and I believe it influences the building of racism and supports the constellation of individual racial complexes as well as collective cultural racial complexes. I think this prejudice is part of the ever-turning circle of racial prejudice, trauma and racial complexes. I believe this cycle begins in the lives of children promoted by the archetypal event of slavery, the intergenerational impact of racial prejudice and unresolved emotions of the complexes. As I sit here reviewing this paper I hear that five police officers in Florence, South Carolina have been shot. What can we learn and share with others about our racial complexes, racial prejudice and cultural trauma? Collective cultural trauma shows itself as having a cultural racial complex that has been formed and nurtured by first slavery, and through centuries of various racist aspects of American life. However, our racial complexes begin within the individual when as children we first encounter trauma.

Even if we do not directly experience a traumatic racial event as a child from the collective, I do believe we will encounter it because our own parents have suffered in this way, and carry the intergenerational pain of cultural trauma due to slavery and its effects. Post-traumatic slave syndrome. Jung's idea of the theory of Opposites has done much in probably an unintended way, to promote American racism. Samuel Kimbles in *Phantom Narratives* has spoken eloquently regarding the racial issues inherent in groups that have their own cultural rituals and rites of passage. One of our landmark rites was the passage of Africans to the Americas as slaves. This event I believe remains a very uncomfortable discussion topic for many Americans even though we have not even began to see deeply into the psychological trauma still being experienced by the descendants of slaves. Slavery was a horrific event that lasted for centuries.

Its influence still lingers and oftentimes dominates our contemporary society. Attempted suppression and repression of our individual and collective racial complexes only give them more energy. Unfortunately, in our unconscious amnesia, we continue to live out our fears through racial complexes expressed most often through racism, racist actions and collective memory trauma.

Jung says, "Complexes are something so unpleasant that nobody in his right senses can be persuaded that the motive forces which maintain them could betoken anything good." These are Jung's words. Can there be any wonder we have avoided within our area of American Jungian Psychology, a depthful discussion of racial complexes, racial prejudice and cultural trauma related to Africanist lineage individuals?

5

A CULTURAL CONSTELLATION

I had most often before Jungian psychology training and practice thought of the constellation as a factor of some heavenly body event. In fact, even within the literature of Jungian psychology there are references to the unconscious and its elements of complexes and archetypes as resembling our night-time sky. Jung's definition of the constellation is as follow:

> This term simply expresses the fact that the outward situation releases a psychic process in which certain contents gather together and prepare for action. When we say that a person is "constellated" we mean that he has taken up a position from which he can be expected to react in a quite definite way. But the constellation is an automatic process which happens involuntarily and which no one can stop of his own accord. The constellated contents are definite complexes possessing their own specific energy. (*A Review of the Complex Theory*, CW 8, para 198)

From psychoanalytical work, I now have a further understanding of constellation in terms of the psychological conscious and unconscious experience of patients, cultural collective instances that occur and my own personal experiences.

I believe the African Holocaust was a genocidal occurrence for millions of Africans, and later African Americans descendants, who followed them. The significance of this event cannot be understated or underestimated as it had been for centuries while it was allowed to thrive economically and socially for whites in the American colonies. I draw on an understanding of what it could mean to have an "outward situation" such as American slavery, and Jim Crow racism that "releases a psychic process," and "in which certain contents gather together and prepare for action."

In the same way that individuals become constellated, I suggest that groups of individuals can become constellated and engaged in human behaviors that reflect a gathering of psychic energy motivated in a particular direction driven by a cultural complex. (Jung, Henderson, Kimbles) Our American collective and Jungian conversations and literature have been empty of discussions regarding the psychological unconscious processes that occurred because of slavery—the African Holocaust and its aftermath. In my discussion of racial complexes, I endeavor to think about this aspect of a cultural complex. I am not removed from my considerations of this process since I, as well as my Africanist ancestors before me, are/were affected by activated racial complexes. I would say that it is partially due to my own racial complex that I write on this particular topic, and search for further understanding in this area of study. Jung noted that we must be taken over, possessed by "something" for which we have a passion. This type of willingness to allow for transcending the ego through a deeper Self is what gives living the greatest amount of emotional satisfaction. Not unlike a complex or archetypal energies, our life passions should claim us. We do not have it—it must have us.

The African Holocaust resulting from the stealing of Africans and being put into enforced slavery supported the development of an unconscious psychic trauma. This initial trauma was the broken off "piece" of psyche within an African cultural consciousness. This is an idea that might appear strange or unacceptable partially because we are so often attuned to thinking about our unconscious selves as holding all of the unconscious rather than it holding us. It also might appear unacceptable because we tend to think of psychological processes as occurring within individuals rather than in the group. An exception to this experience in terms of a cultural collective has been the Jewish Holocaust of the 20th century.

Time, denial and oppression—the latter being one of the key elements of the African Holocaust, has prevented it from being explored in a manner that looks not only at the outer eruption that occurred but also the internal psychic material of the unconscious that affected millions of Africanist people. When there is a shared trauma there is expected to be the development of shared complexes. The millions who were affected would have been expected to have passed their trauma to those following them on an intergenerational manner. It is becoming more obvious with our studies of neuroscience, mirroring neurons, and epigenetics that even two generations of trauma will cause trauma down a line of descendants for many generations to come. The cultural group will experience the psychic trauma that the individual experiences. In my consideration of Africanist individuals arriving on slave ships and all of the millions who descended from them, I cannot be in denial of the possible psychological harm done to them over the centuries. Within our American collective we at first ignored all of the harm done by the Middle Passage. It was at first not even important enough to mention in our history books except the recognition of Europeans such as Columbus for their "discoveries." Then, it merely a few sentences owning that American slavery did in fact exist. The creation of slavery and its resultant cruel racism in American society were integrated into the fiber of every American institution.

Africanist slaves and their descendants have paid on an intergenerational level for this type of institutionalized racism. In the denial of institutionalized racism, the collective was able for many centuries to deny the illegal, inhumane treatment of Africanist people that existed. As I write these words, some seem to want to continue their denial because I think it is difficult to psychologically think on or consider how drastic and severe slavery must have been to those men, women and children who were trapped in this exploitive, punishing system.

I think one reason that this system could last as long as it did was because of the deep, shadowed negation of the true harm done to captured human beings. I think the genocidal aggressive behaviors that were shown during and after slavery and into the Jim Crow era, demanded a complete dark psychological collective shadow to continue to function at the level which it did until the early days of the Civil Rights Movement.

If we can believe in a consciousness that exists in each of us on an individual level, then I would expand the idea of this consciousness to us as human beings within group consciousness. How is one to experience the inner psychic realm of the personal unconscious—the place of complexes within one's cultural group? How is one to be identified with this group and what defines it? I think that in America we have been defined by our skin for so very long that it is hard *not* be have this used as a marker for identification (Brewster, 2017). This is not of itself the major problem. It is rather all that has accompanied the development of *skin culture* and its inseparable attachment to race and racism.

The recognition of one's relatedness to a particular group begins forming at birth, perhaps even soon because we can know even earlier on an archetypal level our psychic selves. If this is true—that we arrive with a psychic self—a memory, an archetypal DNA, then we can very easily find ourselves with the first mirror—our mothers. In this seeing and joining of and with the first Other, we begin to see ourselves. We grow in recognition of ourselves into an identity that continues throughout the lifetime.

A central part of this identity is race recognition—or rather ethnicity recognition. We learn early on to which group we belong and to whom—within our immediate families and our cultural group "families." Within our American collective, this is and has always been supported by our collective consciousness around "race"—though we are one race this was and (is still) largely unacceptable in the broader use of language to speak of or define how we are joined. The word "race" divides us where the word "ethnicity" allows us to keep our unique identities while acknowledging cultural differences.

The cultural complexes of "race" within the Africanist constellation of the unconscious is implicitly tied to the archetypal event of American slavery. I do not believe that we as an ethnic group will ever be able to move away from the unconscious eruptions caused by the African Holocaust. This deeply engraved psychological event has and will continue to define us as a cultural group in almost the same way in which we were physically held captive and defined by slavery. One of the enduring aspects of the complex is that according to Jung, it does not go away. We can work at its transformation and recognizing it when it appears—sometimes, but we will never free ourselves of this psychic aspect of the unconscious. If the complex within the personal unconscious never leaves us then I would anticipate that on a group level we would have the very same experience. I think that we can see this in the behaviors that occur within groups of people when they become "constellated"—whether for good or bad. Whether it is the capturing of African individuals and stacking their bodies on slave ships or Jews into trains headed for Nazi prison/death camps. Both of these catastrophic events show the cultural constellations of a racial complex that included collective Shadow.

I think it is important to address the racialized aspect of our group cultural complex because it is important to the psychological mental health of not just those of African descent living today but also for those who are to follow. It is important because it has been ignored as irrelevant and not mattering in the field of psychology. It is important because it offers validation and recognition to a group within the human community of beings who were categorized for centuries as "beasts" and "breeders." There are those who might disagree and feel it is better to let us stay in the dark, in the shadows. They might believe that it is not important what has occurred before, during or after slavery. All of these periods of time are significant. The lives of Africans before slavery were on their own projectory, having their own teleos. The introjection of European cultural exploitation caused a cultural trauma from which Africanist people have yet to recover.

How do we consider recovery from this type of cultural trauma?

I have found that the absence of widespread discussion within the broad field of Psychology and within the smaller area of Jungian psychology, to inhibit recovery. We cannot recover from that which we are in denial of on an individual or group level.

The American collective's *oppression* as a part of the racial complex extended to every part of the human life—body, language, and mind. I would include the unconscious and its vital importance to finding a healthy *compensation* between ego consciousness and unconscious parts such as complexes and archetypal energies and patterns. It would be very difficult to find this good relationship of compensatory action when oppression is constantly being energized on a group level through enslavement.

How does one imagine this on an unconscious level? We see its result in the lives of the slaves—in their slave narratives. This writing is to help us develop an image, vision, the words to move us out of denial towards an acceptance of more than a possibility but an actualized reality of cultural trauma causing cultural complex constellations. Much of what we have finally learned, don't know or wish to keep shadowed about American slavery seeks its own release as a part of the constellation of the cultural group racial complex. This is the "eruption" that we as an American collective experienced towards the end of the 1950s.

Historical constellations

The American Civil War to end slavery had been over for one hundred years when civil unrest, rebellion and the demand to end Jim Crow grew into a movement that had all the energetic force of a complex taking possession of group egoic consciousness on a massive level. I think the continued civil rights ripples in our lives today of the push for reparations, voter rights laws, and civil liberties reflects this breaking through from the pendulum swing of the archetypal energy of slavery into one of freedom. There was always a cultural collective archetypal "push" by those enslaved to free themselves.

The post-Civil War years were an initial period of hope and expectation in the power of African Americans to obtain their civil rights during Reconstruction. The movement of group archetypal energy that freed slaves also served to heighten the culturally racial demands of whites who had "lost" the Civil War. The Confederacy may have lost to the Yankees on the battlefields but their unconscious selves found expression through the formation of groups such as the Ku Klux Klan. I believe that this initial unconscious engagement with the racial complex emerged in both blacks and whites driven by the archetypal desire for power and control, the former attempting to finally experience the power of having freedom from slavery. The latter in wanting to find some semblance of control of those who had been enslaved and were now "free." The archetypal opposites of freedom and slavery were constellated in post-Civil War in ethnically divided groups. This has been one of our American legacies from which we continue to seek psychological relief.

The history of collective cultural constellations involving race has flowed and ebbed through the centuries. When looking at the length of time of American slavery, it would be natural to expect that the period of time following the emancipation would take more than one hundred years. The enormous eruption of the African Holocaust could not be resolved simply only through an Emancipation Proclamation. In reading some of the newspapers and personal writings of those times, it appears that the hope for a peaceful nation without slavery was very strong. It appeared that very few took into account the psychological trauma of what slavery had caused within the American psyche.

However, we will remember that Jung was not born until 1875, years after the official "freedom" of American slaves. Ideas and theories regarding modern psychology were only beginning with Freud, Janet and Ferenczi. The historical events that led to the group racial complex constellation of the 1960s and 1970s had been forming before the days of these men of modern psychology. However, in the case of Jung, who saw visions and dreams of bloody ocean and a foretelling of death and detailed these in his *Memory, Dreams, Reflections*, African American soldiers fought and died in Germany during World War I. The European cultural battle that spread around the world involved black men who were in wonderment regarding their place in such an engagement in the same way they did in World War II. They reflected on their responsibility to fight for a European and American peace that they were not achieving at home. This doubt regarding their lack of freedom and liberty showed itself through their being demoralized and emotionally unfulfilled while soldering for others while knowing their own despair. It was during the course of both world wars and especially the one of the 1940s, that I believe a group African American racial complex began to be primed ready for constellation in the decade to follow. These men who fought would not have forgotten the archetypal affect of slavery on their family and ancestors before them. How might the archetypal energy of an American Civil War interact with their racial complexes? Since their political, social and economic status had basically not changed very much since that war, nor the Spanish-American War of 1892, how had these engagements to fight for and save the liberties of others—Cubans, activated a racial complex that "remembered" Southern repression and oppression?

Within the context of understanding that complexes are part of a psychological narrative that does not leave us, how might we think of cultural constellation eruptions that would be pre-cursors to much greater racially triggered complexes over time? I think that we have created historical storylines that give us many of the facts of the events of our American wars—fought here and abroad. We have only begun to consider in our literature and discussions the psychological, psychic and intergenerational trauma caused by a cultural complex that is driven by raciality and *never* within the context of American warfare. Complexes survive and continue to exist due to emotionally painful past associations. How might this appear to be lived out in the behavior or those who had experienced war? What is the psychological conflict of opposites within the psyche striving for clarity regarding risking one's life to save that of another who under different circumstances—on American soil might be attempting to end your life? Might this cause dissociation, a strong emotion of rage, a deep sadness? When thinking of the stress of war, being a soldier and what we understand now regarding post-traumatic stress disorder, how is this applicable to African American soldiers fighting a psychological battle on two fronts? I do not believe that the racial discrimination they experienced while in military training would be forgotten. The white privilege they suffered and others enjoyed because of skin color rather than ability could be forgotten. The African American soldier fighting on foreign soil for the freedom of others was very aware of how limited his own life was by racism.

This added an addition burden to his life while fighting for others who would one day go back to enjoying basic human rights that he would find difficult to experience in his own home, city and country.

The outside wars on foreign soil was one contributing factor that set the external circumstance for African Americans to evaluate and compare their own American lives ever more deeply within a negative racial complex. The archetypal energies of shadow, slavery and freedom gathered force and became more obvious at the beginning of the 20th century.

We think of ourselves and come to know ourselves from both ego and the unconscious. This being the case, African Americans could begin to see by the turn of the 20th century that the freedom and the results of it that they had believed would be the beginning of new lives was not to be obtained in the way they may have imagined. The psychological ground for American collective thinking was heightened in 1915 with the creation of the film *Birth of a Nation*. This film paid homage to the rights, privileges and superiority of whites over black Americans. It received praise by many for the clear statement of racial bias it promoted. The images of blacks being lynched and terrorized by whites in hoods added to the collective American shadow of racism with a constellation of a white racial complex. The film *Birth of a Nation* could give back a sense of power and control lost in the Civil War—a belief in the wholeness of white supremacy. The broken psychic trauma of the white racial complex could have a place to find solace. Suppressed anger and rage directed at blacks could find expression in the constellated acting out behaviors of the white racial complex.

The white cultural revolution took shape in a new century. "In the very first year of the new century more than 100 African Americans were lynched, and before the outbreak of World War I the number for the century had soared to more than 1,1000" (p. 312) It has returned in our 21st century with some of the familiar parts of itself on display—voter suppression, violent racist language against people of color—black and brown, promotion of the supremacy of white people and a rage that can kill.

The years between world wars—we might think of them as the resting period, non-active period of the cultural complex with one exception—African Americans were continuing to feel the effects of a cultural white racial complex that reflected the poor education of black children and discrimination against them in housing and jobs. The creation of the Negro Association for the Advance of Colored People (NAACP), formed in 1907 struggled to promote equality in American life for all black people. In all areas of African American life, racism showed itself—even socially. Decades later the struggle continued. In 1939, Marion Anderson was refused the right to sing at Constitution Hall by the Daughters of the American Revolution. Instead, she was able to give a performance at the Lincoln Memorial to a crowd of 75,000 people.

The 1940s saw the energetic build up and showcasing of racial complexes. The Second World War was to reproduced itself as the archetypal engagement of nations fighting one another on a cultural/tribal level. This continued for African Americans and whites on a collective level in the years prior to America's entry into the war. One of the worse events that showed the racially activated complexes of African Americans and whites was the "race riot" of Detroit that took place in June of 1943. The initial engagement was due to a fistfight between two men—one black, one white.

> The altercation rapidly spread to involve several hundred people of both races. Wild rumors, as usual, swept through the town. Within a few hours blacks and whites were fighting thought most of Detroit. When the governor hesitated to declare martial law and call out troops, whites began to roam the streets, burning blacks' cars and beating large numbers of black people. Nothing effective was done to bring order out of the chaos until president Roosevelt proclaimed a state of emergency and sent 6,000 soldiers to patrol the city. At the end of more than thirty hours of rioting 25 African Americans and 9 whites had been killed, and property valued at several hundred thousand dollars had been destroyed. (Franklin and Moss, 1997, p. 453)

The other area of a fierce energetic conflict was in the area of the American military. As America prepared to industrialize itself for entry into the war, discrimination against blacks was obvious at the inclusion of them into not only war preparations but also the military.

> As African Americans saw wages skyrocket at plants holding large defense contracts and no change in the rigid antiblack policy in industry, they developed a program for drastic action. In January 1941, A. Philip Randolph, president of the Brotherhood of Sleeping Car Porters, advanced the idea of 50,000 to 1000,000 blacks marching on Washington and demanding that their government do something to ensure the employment of blacks in defense industries ... as plans

were laid for the march, high government official became alarmed. ((Franklin and Moss, 1997, p. 436)

The pull and push of political racial ambivalence towards African Americans continued until President Roosevelt issued an executive order stating there would be no discrimination against black employment in the defense industries or the federal government. Even with this presidential order, the selection of African Americans into the military forces was slow and biased. The creation of the Selective Service Act of 1940 gradually brought more men and women into the armed services.

However, as in the past, racism called for segregated units. The navy did not begin more fully integrate until 1942.

Overall, racism continued in the all arms forces though more and even stronger military rules were put into place to force the decrease in racial prejudice. This even extended to the building of 14 war ships named after African Americans such as Harriet Tubman. Racism survived as did the racial complexes that guaranteed its behavior in the simplest of ways to the most insulting.

> On military posts the situation was scarcely better. Several commanding officers forbade the reading of black newspapers, and there were instances in which black newspapers were taken from newsboys or soldiers and burned. At many camps transportation for African-American soldiers was most unsatisfactory. They were frequently forced to wait until buses had been loaded with white soldiers before they were permitted to board them. At post exchanges they were segregated and given inferior merchandise. Theaters and other entertainment facilities were frequently set apart, and accommodations for blacks were below the standard of those provided for whites. The War Department took cognizance of the discrimination against African-American soldiers in its order of July 8, 1944, which forbade racial segregation in recreational and transportation facilities. A veritable storm of protest arose in the South as the order was made known. (Franklin and Moss 1997, p. 446)

In his State of the Union Address of January, 1941, President Franklin Roosevelt gave what became known as his Four Freedom speech. This speech was given as a sign of support for America's allies in the war effort. The four freedoms: speech, worship of the God of choice, freedom from want and from fear, were not believed by African American soldiers to extend to them and their military lives. The question became the same one as before. How can I imagine myself fighting for the fundamental freedom of others in a foreign war while I cannot have these same freedoms at home?

I would imagine that this would remain in support of the activation of a cultural black racial complex duplicating the initial broken off piece of the trauma of slavery—broken in spirit, identity and from family. These became the repeated psychic markers of the racial complex seen in the behaviors of African American soldiers and enlisted men who served in the military for most of the years of their service. But the war had caused a shift in consciousness that was soon to be realized by the American collective.

The war had created a climate in which substantial gains could be make, but the very nature of the emergency imposed certain restraints that could no longer be justified after 1945 … The executive branch of the federal sensitive to both domestic and foreign pressures, exerted considerable influence in eradicating the gap between creed and practice in American democracy. ((Franklin and Moss 1997, p. 461)

At first it appeared that with the war years behind America, the racial tensions of the first half of the 20th century would dissipate. As time came to reveal, the cultural conflicts between whites and blacks re-emerged as the latter once more grew in understanding that they would not gain the political, social or economic liberties that whites had for centuries. The conscious drive of African countries to gain their freedom from colonization, spread its influence to New York through the United Nations and in 1957, Ghana was the first African country to be admitted to the UN with all rights as an independent country without colonial ties. Once again the African American cultural collective saw itself reflected in the freedom of others while viewing itself without such freedom. The war years had passed for almost a decade when in 1953 through 1957 civil rights passed to insure more voting and civil liberties for blacks. They proved insufficient to counter the archetypal energy and constellated racial complexes expressing frustration, anger and dismay over the on-going lack of reciprocity from whites in having African American citizens share in the American wealth of truly being an American.

By the time of the first demonstration by Dr. Martin Luther King in 1956, the African American psyche as primed for a radical change that I believe grew from an archetypal core of the demand for treatment as a human being not an inferior former slave.

6

ARCHETYPE, SHADOW, COMPLEX

Archetype

The relationship of archetype, shadow and complex is an enjoined one that can involve our basic human nature, psychic dimension and behavioral environment engagements. In discussing the racial complex within this chapter the focus is on the interaction between archetypal energies and energies of the archetype emerging as in individuals and groups.

Jung began defining archetypes at different times as he began to more clearly realize their characteristics. Initially, Jung began to research and understand archetypes through his own personal dream work and his work with schizophrenic patients at the Burgholzli Hospital. In 1919 he first began to use the term archetype in his writings:

> In this "deeper" stratum we also find the a priori inborn forms of "intuition namely the archetypes of perception and apprehension which are the necessary a priori determinants of all psychic processes. (*Collected Works*, vol. 8, para 270)

Jung's description of the archetype has varied throughout his writings. He has spoken of the archetype as a primordial image. (*CW* vol. 8, para.277)

Jolande Jacobi (1974) observes ways that Jung's use of the word "meant all the mythologems, all the legendary or fairy-tale motifs, etc. which concentrate universally human modes of behavior into images, or perceptible patterns" (p. 33)

Jungians who worked with Jung seeking to deepen his writing on the archetypes included Jolande Jacobi. In *Complex Archetype Symbol in the Psychology of C.G. Jung*, the author says the following:

> It is impossible to give an exact definition of the archetype, and the best we can hope to do is to suggest its general implications by "talking around" it. For

the archetype represents a profound riddle surpassing our rational comprehension … No direct answer can be given to the questions of whence the
archetype comes and whether or not it is acquired. (p. 31)

In the discussion of the archetype I would like to turn to African thought. It is
important to broaden the view of how one might think of the archetype within a
cultural realm. Jung spoke and wrote of the universality of the archetypes; however,
when this was in terms of Africanist people, the hierarchy of consciousness placed
them at the bottom. In sharing the quote below I want to introduce another way of
thinking about archetype within an inclusive contextual model that can be universal.
The following essay is "Foundations for an African American Psychology" by Thomas
Parham. It is a description of the African mind-soul-body connection that the author
believes underpins African American psychology for individuals from this culture. The
Kemetic is an Egyptian one taken from the historical tradition of consciousness.

> In ancient Kemetic metaphysics, the psyche, or soul, comprised seven interrelated
> dimensions. First the psyche was composed of the KA, or the physical structure of
> an individual's humanity. This body each individual inhabited, without spirit or
> energy, would deteriorate into those earthly elements from which it came at the
> end of one's life. The second dimension of the psyche was the BA, or the breath
> of life. This energy or life force was believed to be transmitted by the Creator and
> ancestors into each individual and was seen as the essence of all things that have
> life. The third dimension of the psyche was represented by the KHABA, which
> represented emotion and motion. Motion in this regard related to the natural
> order of things, including rhythmic patterns characterized by blood circulation.
> The fourth dimension of the psyche was the AKHU, which represented the seat
> of intelligence or the capacity for thought and mental perception. It was char-
> acterized by judgment, analysis, and mental reflection. The fifth dimension is the
> SEB, or eternal soul. This element of the psyche was thought to manifest itself
> once an individual reached adolescence or puberty and was characterized by the
> self-creative power/ability to reproduce one's own kind. The sixth dimension of
> the psychic nature was the PUTAH, and it represented the union of the brain
> with the conscious mind … mental maturity. The seventh dimension of the
> psyche nature is known as the ATMU. It was considered the Divine or eternal
> soul. (*Handbook for African American Psychology*, 2009, pp. 8–9)

In the realm of soul, psyche, the divine, it is not necessary to create divisions that
create an artificial segregation. The natural order or rhythm of the joining of the
human and the divine I believe happens in an organic way because this is how we are
naturally made as humans.

As African Americans in search of not only the existential and reality-based necessity
of freedom, there is the need to remedy, to heal psychological trauma. This remedy in
following Jungian psychology thinking will emerge from whatever makes up the
poison. What is its' nature? Since a large part of the nature of racism has been its

insistence on the inferiority of black people, it could follow that the remedy would be the inclusion of ideas, thinking and an insistence on language from an African source that works towards compensation—a balancing of the Opposites in support of the superiority and value of Africanist people.

> The first president of the American Psychological Association, G. Stanley Hall, theorized that Africans, Indians, and Chinese were members of "adolescent races" and in the stage of "incomplete growth" (Richards, 1997) and that therefore it was Western psychology's role and responsibility to save the adolescent races from the liabilities of freedom. (p. 38)

As the European influenced American psychologies grew it attracted to itself the racism of the white cultural collective. It is not unexpected that Stanley Hall and other early Americans of the psychoanalytical movement would blend in America's own ideas regarding raciality to ideas on psychology to those ancestors stolen from Africa. The early profession of psychologists and psychiatrists had begun in its early days to incorporate racism into the young field of American psychology.

> In 1797, Dr. Benjamin Rush, the reputed "father of American psychiatry," declared that the color of Black was caused by a congenital disease akin to leprosy. The only evidence of a cure was when the skin turned white. (p. 38)

In the continuing efforts to justify slavery, the psychiatric medical profession added their contribution to American society's social climate and literature:

> The cultural lens used by those developing the field had been so fractured that healthy, efficacious behaviors on the part of Black people were perceived and defined as insane. In 1851, Dr. Samuel Cartwright published an article in a professional journal of his time claiming that he had discovered two new mental diseases peculiar to Black people: (1) drapetomania, which caused Black people to have the uncontrollable urge to run away from their slave captors and (2) dyaesthesia aethiops, evidenced by disobedience, answering disrespectfully, and refusing to work. The commonly prescribed cures were beating them mercilessly and forcing the captive to undertake even more taxing and difficult labor. (p. 38)

I provide readings like the above quote so that we are able to compare and consider the various possibilities for how we might evaluate the idea and experience of not only the archetype but also psychological healing (represented by the Asclepius serpent), and the foundational philosophical source of our beliefs regarding healing. I illustrate the thinking regarding Africanist people within the field of psychology from its early days because this is a part of the "poison" that must be inspected with an eye to considering the "remedy." It may not have been considered a poison by the early developers of American psychology but was and has proven to be that for the African Diaspora. Jungian psychology was not immune to this and Jung was a close colleague and invited guest of G. Stanley Hall when the former came to St. Elizabeth's Hospital to conduct his dream work research on 15 African Americans men in 1912(?). (Brewster, 2017) Jung traveled to Washington D.C. at that time to prove the universality of his archetypes and their existence as the collective unconscious. His point being that even African Americans and their dreams showed that ethnicity was not a prohibitive factor as far the collective unconscious was concerned. We all belonged to the collective unconscious and it belonged to all of us.

In *The Religious Function of the Psyche* (1997), author and Jungian analyst Lionel Corbett's, descriptions of the archetype are very similar to those whom I refer to as Kemetic and Jung's own considerations of the unconscious and what it is and how it shows itself in the form of the archetypal. Corbett states:

> Therefore the religious attitude to the psyche regards attention to introspectively obtained material, such as dreams, visions, creative products, emotional distress, fantasy or simply reflection on personal history, as a valid spiritual pursuit if the transpersonal or archetypal underpinnings of such events are recognized. This attitude relies on a contentious axiom of the depth psychological approach. (p. 5)

It is not uncommon to read in Jungian literature a dismissal of some parts of Jung's theory of the archetypes. In my own writing, I have tried to clarify where his theories of the collective unconscious have not been generally supportive of Africanist people due to the racism attached to his proposed idea regarding levels of consciousness—black people being inferior and at the bottom.

I am interested in seeing more of the Africanist linguistic and philosophic roots of the archetype, to understand the language of these African forefathers as they consider that which is a universality for all—as Jung himself said. As the archetypes and their energies show themselves in the cultural clothes of their times, how best can the remedy salve of an un-maligned cultural heritage be applied to centuries long racial trauma?

Shadow

The shadow as an archetype connected with the individual as well as an aspect of the collective at large has become more widely known. When Jung first began his discussion of the shadow he considered this a necessary element of the personal unconscious. "The archetypes most clearly characterized from the empirical point of view are those which have the most frequent and the most disturbing influence on the ego. These are the *shadow*, the *anima*, and the *animus*" (*CW* vol. 9ii, para 13) Jung continues to say that the shadow archetype was the most accessible to the ego.

In a further description of the shadow Jung says, "The shadow is a moral problem that challenges the whole ego-personality, for no one can become conscious of the shadow without considerable moral effort." (CW vol. 9ii, para 14)

The details that Jung provides naming the

"dark characteristics—that is, the inferiorities constituting the shadow—emotional nature, a kind of autonomy, and accordingly an obsessive or, better, possessive quality … Affects occur usually where adaption is weakest, and at the same time they reveal the reason for its weakness, namely a certain degree of inferiority and the existence of a lower level of personality. On this lower level with it uncontrolled or scarcely controlled emotions one behaves more or less like a primitive, who is not only the passive victim of his affects but also singularly incapable of moral judgment. (CW vol. 9ii, para 15)

Jung having said the above regarding the shadow later spoke of projection of the shadow onto others. In the course of time this shadow projection arrived upon Africanist people—this was especially true in Jungian dream work where all people of color were considered the shadow and having negative features of the shadow. Jung's reference to moral judgment especially relevant because in the text *Encountering Jung on Evil*, edited by Murray Stein, Jung in an essay from the *Collected Works*, vol. 10, "A Psychological View of Conscience," discusses the relationship between conscience and morality. He suggests that a choice is given when deciding whether to commit an amoral act. He imagines that he is suggesting that due to his lowered level of consciousness the "primitive" will be unable to choose morality. I think there is more to be said about the paradoxical nature of the Africanist being considered incapable of moral judgment. This will be discussed in Chapter 10.

In my discussion of the racial complex I propose that the archetypal core of this complex is the shadow. I believe that more than one type of archetypal energy can interface with this shadow but I believe it has dominance at the core center of the complex. My writing in *The Racial Complex* has explored the negative aspect of the racial complex. What might be the positive end? I consider safety and preservation of life as one part of the Africanist cultural collective racial complex. It is interesting that even when considering the positive end of the spectrum of this complex, the language is about defense.

The negative racist nature of the racial complex has been so intensely realized, lived, and acted out in America that it is difficult to imagine a positive spectrum end to this complex. This could, of course, be related to my own racial complex activation that limits my ego's perspective. My only context for the positive or negative end of the complex's activation can be shown within the clinical setting. In those moments of transference and phenomenological experiences, this complex as with any other can present and influence the work. The shadow in all clinical work is also waiting to be revealed and engaged with—to be revealed, in service of deepening the psychological work of both analyst and analysand.

The individual as well as the collective shadow is discussed in the *Introduction to Encountering Jung: Jung on Evil*, author Stein says:

The first duty of the ethically minded person is, from Jung's psychological perspective, to become as conscious as possible of his or her own shadow. The shadow is made up of the personality's tendencies, motives, and traits that a person considers shameful for one reason or another and seeks to suppress or actually represses unconsciously. It they are repressed, they are unconscious and are projected into others. When this happens, there is usually strong moral indignation and the groundwork is lad for a moral crusade. Filled with right-eous indignation, persons can attack others for perceiving in them what is unconscious shadow in themselves, and a holy war ensues. (p. 17)

Stein says the following in response to the question "What is the source of the deed, the "raw fact." which one judges to be evil? His response follows:

For example, war is a common human event that is often judged to be evil. Is war-making native to the human species? It would seem that war-making is intrinsic to part of human nature … human beings seem to have a kind of aggressiveness toward one another and a tendency to seek domination over others, as well as a strong desire to protect their own possessions and families or their tribal integrity, which added together lead inevitably to conflict and to war. Some would say that war is a natural condition of humanity as a species, and it would be hard to dispute this from the historical record. Is making war not archetypal? Does this not mean that evil is deeply woven into the fabric of human existence? (pp. 11–12)

If we will fight with one another on a one to one level as well as in massive wars, is there a way to see one another's shadow more clearly, and once we do pull back the negative projections? Does the shadow projection get withdrawn first as we learn that the things we find intolerable are actually a part of ourselves? From this are we then better able to see the Other?

In the course of reading Jung's writings I have indicated several places where I feel his shadow lightens and his language becomes painfully racially charged in respect to Africanist people. The "lingering shadow" of questions surrounding Jung's anti-Semitic shadow is the theme of *Jung and the Shadow of Anti-Semitism* (2002), an anthology of essays edited by Aryeh Maidenbaum. In his Introduction to the book he says, "Whatever the reasons for Jung's attitudes and actions, he displayed in the midst of a dangerous and frightening time, a regrettable lack of political and personal con-sequences of his written spoken words." In different narrative accounts, with a view to Jung's life before, during and after the Second World War, a number of writers express their opinions including Ann Belford Ulanov in "Scapegoating: The Double Cross." She opens her essay: "Scapegoating and anti-Semitism are not subjects we can speak about objectively. We can only speak of them out of suffering—unconsciousness, abysmal pain and terror, rage and guilt, and a persistent to glimpse a way through their thickets of fear, sadism, violence, and despair" (p. 98). I appreciate her words that so clearly articulates these feelings and feelings for myself and those of my own cultural collective which has experienced an ethnic holocaust.

As we slowly move into the 21st century, we as Jungians do not leave behind Jung's experiences. This appears to be as he wanted it—his life, dream work and all else was a path to share with us how we could learn a way of life that was spirited, divine and in this way psychological. Jungian literary writers with noted exceptions have chosen to not address Jung's racially negative references to Africanist people. However, Ulanov discusses this in terms of Jung and anti-Semitism.

Ulanov writes:

> Jung missed on the feeling and sensate levels—in terms of his typology his own inferior functions—the reality of the evil being visited upon the Jews. He wrote and spoke about racial characteristics, both during and after the war, in a way that was bound to further inflame the persecution of a whole people. Caught in his own emotions about he Wotan archetype, and his own resentments against Freudian analysis, he did not see the harm he himself was causing. (p. 106)

I think of Ulanov's writing and consider Jung being "possessed" by the archetypal energy of the god of war, his complex is constellated, several of the book's essay writers seem to feel it is the father complex and his own shadow which prevents him from seeing the evil of the Nazi Socialist Party. I don't see the same type of energetic force at work when he focuses on Africanist individuals or the cultural group. The negative racialized comments and theories are forthright and appear to be stated with a certainty that leaves no doubt. Africanist people will be the scapegoat of some of his theories. Jung's theorizing appeared almost matter of fact. During the years that Hitler was building his "thousand years" Nazi empire, African Americans were engaged in their struggle against Jim Crow in every facet of their lives. Jung's theories meant little or nothing to them on the broad landscape of survival. The casting of his shadow and its darkening during this time period as related to Africanist people fell short of reaching them. However, it did add to the overall texture of American psychology racism.

This lack of contact was perhaps partly due to the issue of American eugenics, the economic effects of the Depression and the continued lynching of black people. There was no time to consider Jungian psychology theory when survival was an everyday deadly struggle. Unfortunately, there is a correlation between eugenics, racism and the politics of 1930s Germany and America that worked to undermine the social efforts of African Americans during that time period.

Francis Galton in 1883 began using the word eugenics as way to describe his theory or "science of improving the stock." In his book, *Inquiries into Human Faculties* (1883), he expressed his belief in the betterment of the races through genetic selection.

Anthropologist Roger Pearson began in 1991 through his writings to repeat and enhance Galton's theories. In *The Nazi Connection: Eugenics, American Racism, and Germany National Socialism*, author Stefan Kuhl says of Pearson:

> Pearson informs his readers that the original intention of eugenics was 'clearly and unabashedly the goal of breeding a more gifted race." According to Pearson, eugenicists believed that Europeans as well as other gifted races were

already of distinguished genetic capability, but that "just as races differed genetically, so breeding groups of individuals with nations and regional populations might also differ genetically." (p. 4)

This collectively popular and psychologically damaging line of illogical reasoning gained strength in America and was of interest within the scientific and general population for almost the first half of the 20th century. Even though eugenics became known in Britain and Germany, of course the focus within the United States was on those determined to be "feebleminded" and "unfit" (p. 16). This was mainly African Americans. Laws that prohibited the marriage between different ethnic groups—white and black—were seen as a way to keep the white race pure and to prevent what was known as "race suicide" (p. 16).

I consider the eugenics movement one that gained strength from a white racial complex that archetypally gained power and influence. The German Nazi race policies against the Jewish people were a part of the archetypal energetic force that was planning genocide in Europe through sterilization and that would lead to mass murders and the Second World War. It seemed that American eugenicists were mostly concerned not so much with being anti-Semitic, though this certainly an aspect of their programs, their main focus was on skin color as a determiner of racial superiority. When American eugenicists began to protest the worsening treatment of Jews in America, the German eugenicists responded in the following manner through a German publication. It highlights the hypocrisy of the American eugenicists while showing their main focus of racial discrimination:

> In 1937, the *Preussiche Zeitung* claimed, under the title "The 'cruel German racial theory' and its comparisons abroad," that "liberal circles' that criticize German race laws as an "intervention in human freedom" overlooked the fact that a "state which can be seen as democratic" had its own race laws. The newspaper informed its readers that in thirty states in the United States, marriage between blacks and whites was forbidden. It also referred to the strict segregation between whites and blacks and pointed out that lynching of ethnic minorities was a phenomenon not found in Germany. (p. 98)

The Germans were well aware of American racial policies against blacks since both of their eugenics programs had been in cooperative operation for decades. "In Nazi propaganda after the mid-1930s, the United States became the main point of reference, by reason of its specific combination of ethnic and eugenic racism as well as the extent to which information on Americans eugenics was available in Germany" (p. 99).

After the bombing of Pearl Harbor, American eugenicists stopped their relationship with Germany. It took this act of aggression—coming from Japan—to sever the racist based cooperation between the two countries.

"The pride with which scientists in the 1910s, 1920s, and 1930s referred to themselves as eugenicists has evaporated. After World War II, eugenicists described themselves as 'population scientists,' 'human geneticists,' 'psychiatrists,' 'sociologists,' 'anthropologists,' and 'family politicians' in an attempt to avoid eugenics terminology." (p. 105) The unique brand of racism developed by the eugenics movement in America evolved under different organization names and under the guidance of those who continued to believe in "ethnic purity." (p. 6)

Complex

The characteristics of the complex according to Jung almost demands that it be purposeful in its own aims—there is basically no direction from ego consciousness until the complex becomes consistently known over time. Another feature is its ability to cause the person under its influence to forget—to have amnesia as to how it overtakes the thinking function during an episode of "blankness" or dissociation. In what appears to be watching from a distance the individual under the complex activation influence can observe what is occurring but may feel powerless to act while experiencing stress. One of the primary features of the experience of being "consumed" by the effects of a complex is that one becomes emotion "dominated." This type of domination can release feelings and emotions causing behaviors that prove damaging to the self as well as others.

In my own interests as to the emotional and behavioral aspects of what occurs to us when we are caught in a complex I think about not only the individual but also the group.

Since the culture of African Americans and their response to the impact of living in America since slavery days, it appears relevant to explore how social groups respond to one another when showing signs of being constellated by complex and archetypal energies.I return here to discussing the core of the complex. One author, Hans Dieckmann has specified that there is not only one psychic energy but several available at a time for usage, within the human dimension, as we engage with material from the unconscious. There is an overlapping of psychic material and as the ego encounters this material any number of inner forces are at work.

In Hans Dieckmann's *Complexes: Diagnosis and Therapy in Analytical Psychology*, the author say:

> It is clear that a complex always consists of a mixture of collective and personal material, and the farther its parts are dissociated from the ego complex, the more mythological the character they take on. Here I am advancing the hypothesis that even in the core of the complex—even in the case of a great dissociation from the ego-complex—elements of very early personal experience are enmeshed and must be taken into account in the structure of the core. For the most part, it is difficult to reconstruct them clinically since they lie outside the realm of voluntary recall in the very earliest periods of life. (p. 45)

Dieckmann is addressing the individual but as I relate his hypothesis the cultural group member. I refer back to the previous discussion of group members of the Nazi Socialist Party and neo-Nazis who have followed them since then. Individuals from this latter group after leaving the party and discussing their conversion to this group speak of their isolation and desire to become a part of something that was not like their early childhood involving no attached relationship with parents.

As we observe the behavior both verbal and physical of those who express their rage against people of color, we see in these behaviors something in the psyche of the individual who now in an enactment with their cultural group, are able to return to childhood days. They generally address the loneliness they felt and now in joining the group can feel the security that had been missing earlier on in life. Loneliness is a part of being human and a part of maturing is learning to reconcile one's self to these periods of being without the company of another. The constellation of the negative aspect of the racial complex appears when through group actions individuals are fueled and encouraged by the energy field of the group. This can happen in any situation—the rise and exit of archetypal energies that bear the purpose of what the moment demands. Jung says, "The archetype always meets the need of the moment." (*CW* vol. 5ii, p. 450)

If this is true then we will continue to have moments where because of a particular complex—within in this case either individual or group, there will be an expression of their anger and rage due to the ethnicity of another. I think in addition to the false rationales given to the endurance of American slavery, that it was and has been the constellation of the racial complex that charged by bitterness over what the Other has, or wants, becomes enraged.

What becomes of white rage that expects because of the "inferiority" of the "Other" it should be entitled? When we discuss white privilege today is this not what we are addressing? The "Negro" racial complex of which Jung spoke has lived in the white cultural group of the American psyche for hundreds of years. What are the features of this cultural white racial complex?

When we see the history of slavery, the Civil War and all that followed, how might we consider the type of constellation that could be forthcoming? I think that archetypal energies of both white and black seek expression. Jung when speaking of the Americans (he meant whites) and what they were experiencing with their complex, it was the "colored" man under his skin. How might this show up, be experienced in the white cultural group in terms of their relationship with blacks? Are the years of Jim Crow and all forms of racism that even continue until today, a sign of this irritation—this need to scratch and rid oneself of the "problem"? A good amount of black literature in the past has referred to the American collective sense of Africanist people as being the "problem." In fact, W.E.B. DuBois has specifically discussed this shadow projection onto blacks.

Over time—centuries, as perhaps the compensatory nature of the unconscious sought more balance (social justice), within the sociological field, and so the waves of racial disruptions of Africanist people seeking freedom began and continued through the Emancipation Proclamation. However, the racial complex with all of its negative associations developed, and the archetypal shadow grew darker and consciousness appeared to recede into a place of deeper regression. Imagine the darkness of the American psyche as millions of people were surviving in an archetypal genocidal pattern colored by the nigredo of unconscious psychic material and conscious learned experiences that were renewed over centuries. This *is* frightening in those moments of intense racial witnessing at the death of another black person to see how we in our 21st century collective memory keep trying to repress the shadowed material of racism as it emerges again and again in the form of unconscious complex material that has been repressed and that has never or rarely seen the light of day before. The nature of the repression and our desire and inability to face our collective shadow can confront us in more than one way in terms of the complexes and their constellation. I think this is why some racial eruptions appear so unexpected and heartbreaking. Dieckmann (p. 9)

> Hence complexes belong to the fundamental structure of the psyche and place us human beings in conflicts which it is our task to suffer and to resolve. In Jung's view, suffering in human life is never an illness as such; rather it presents the opposite pole to happiness, and the one is unthinkable without the other. A complex becomes pathogenic only when it is repressed, suppressed, or denied in that we think that we don't have it. A complex turns into a negative and disruptive element in the psyche only due to the ego-complex's insufficient capacity to face it.

How many centuries was it a collective avoidance, repression, suppression, a denial to confront racism in a full frontal way? Eventually, we had a civil war that briefly caused a shift on both a conscious as well as unconscious level. However, the white cultural racial complex with its ego observer that may have suffered defeat on the southern battlefields faded back in the shadow and regained its power through the rule of Jim Crow. The emergence of the Black Power Movement and the use of specifically these words say much not only about the conscious efforts of the individuals engaged at the time but also about the unconscious *movement, power* and *blackness* of complexes and shadow. This is the level of energy required to confront centuries of repression and denial to meet it directly. The unconscious continuation of racism in the American collective met its' conflictual partner in the deepening of consciousness of this black movement. The display of the racial complexes and the centuries of suffering acted out in our daily lives took our attention for several years.

How is this continued violence acted out in our lives today? We call them by new names: micro-aggressions, seeking legislative power in the halls of justice. Black people are killed, most often by law enforcement where there is a charge of negative racial intent to do bodily harm. The idea of using police to cause harm to Africanist people is not a new one and has existed in the American collective for a very long time. To protect and serve has most often times never been considered amongst African Americans to mean protect and serve *us*. When we think about what police are protecting we know from our history that they are protecting the property of those in power. From the earliest days of slavery, this would have been the land and those belonging to the land—black people. I'm not certain that this lived experience is not still a part of some aspect of the white racial complex having to do with control of the black Other.

The power of the slave owner was shared and executed by the overseer—it was their job to police Africanist people. How has this continued to live in that unconscious place of psyche in our 21st-century lives? How do we justify the ongoing murder of black people at the hands of the police? What is happening on an unconscious level, within the personal unconscious, within the archetypal unconscious? I believe that the deeper psychic structures that we have come to understand better through neuroscience helps give us some guidance in considering these questions. I also think that the see-saw movement of psyche can move bi-directionally, that is does not seek only the good or only the bad. History has shown us that we can and will live with the "bad," with evil for a very long time.

The workings of energetic pulses, spirited forms, archetypal intensity and more rise to our consciousness and keep us moving in old patterns much longer than we would like. This is the compulsion and autonomy of the complexes and archetypes. Dieckmann (p. 15)

> A complex turns pathological in one of only two ways. First it can draw excessive energy to itself, which we can understand from our (personal) developmental history, because it contains very early, deep feelings of love or hate also linked with equally deep fears and aggressive impulses. Second, it can become pathological if split off and isolated from the rest of the psyche as a consequence of these overpowering energies and the excessive accumulation of associations and amplifications they bring about.

What does century old-hate look like when repeated in the unconscious on an inter-generational level and finally exploding into ego consciousness on a collective level?

When we think about the true nature of complexes we can learn to anticipate how they exist as a part of our human lives and see the possibility of redemption and healing through their "prospective character" as noted by Dieckmann in his text:

> There are complexes that have never entered consciousness and that therefore have never been repressed. These complexes arise primarily from the collective unconscious. The unconscious is, of course, the matrix out of which conscious-ness arises in the first place. Thus the collective unconscious represents an auton-omous functional complex with an inherent, primary structure in which, as in a seed, the typical development and maturational possibilities of the human psyche are latent. The collective unconscious has a prospective character since, by creat-ing the images in the cores of the complexes, it is in the position of linking them with drive energies and imparting meaning and direction to them. (p. 10)

The meaning and direction that have been the drivers of the racial complexes have I believe resided on the negative end of the complex—the pathological side. When Jung wrote of how all in the psyche is there in service of good psychological well-being, I believe this is true. I also believe that we are in the struggle on many levels, to deal with our paradoxical lives, the oppositional internal and external rages that we must endure and the ego's need for supremacy over our dark, shadow unconscious material. When we cannot, for whatever reason, bring ourselves to explore this material then we find ourselves at a loss. This loss as we have seen over the centuries is both on a deeply felt individual as well as collective level. The racism that impacted Africanist people for centuries cut into the psychic fabric lives of all Americans. However, unfortunate as it may be, at this time, there does not appear to be a collective opening for thinking on individuals of a white cultural lineage and their suffering. Actually isn't this what the Trump presidency has brought us to in our society's national conversation? It seems that the more whites look into a historical context of white privilege—demanding more, to make America great again, the more blacks look into their own historical context of the African Holocaust. Where there has already been centuries of privilege, the compensatory movement of psyche and group ego consciousness would be in the direction of certainly not less social equality but rather much more.

Dieckmann says in continuing his discussion of the pathology of the complex:

> Then like a dictator who arrogates all power to himself, the complex tends to suppress and repress everything that will not fit in its frame of reference ... (p. 15)

As we think about the racial complex of an American psyche, we think about how our complexes seek release in acts of aggression encouraged by political events. Author Sukey Fontelieu in her opening chapter says the following in *The Archetypal Pan in America: Hypermasculinity and Terror*:

> In the US, since the turn of the millennium, violent attacks perpetrated by homegrown shooters, radical Jihadists, and rapists have increase in tandem with a rise in a type of hypermasculine leadership, a neoconservative undercurrent in the country that resurfaced as the Tea Party and is now in full display under the current President of the United States, Donald Trump. (p. 1)

Every action that we take as individuals and members of our cultural group is a reflection of an unconscious motivation brought forth into the light of consciousness. It appears, however, that there are things we still cannot tolerate bringing into full conscious daylight such as the killings within our collective due to a lack of gun control policies.

Fontelieu asks, "Why is there no rational response to gun control reform in a nation where gun sales increase dramatically with each incidence of violence?" (p. 1)

In my thinking about this question and the American cultural complex, I find that I'm willing to ask more questions regarding the cultural ground upon which our 21st-century American lives were built. It may seem too repetitive to say how the founding of American consciousness was based on the blood of others. That there needed to be created an Other to satisfy the unacknowledged, unclaimed inner shadow that found and began to destroy Native Americans and other people of color. In remembering this part of history, we can perhaps begin to have more of an understanding for the need to remember our psychological undertow that swirls around in the unconscious repressing, hiding and keeping us blind throughout the repetition of destructive actions. If we can accept that it is most difficult to live with our shadow, complexes and sometime the archetypal energies that flow uncontrollably through us, then this might enable us to put away our guns.

It might enable us to question the need for arming our police forces as if they are going to war and fighting a "foreign" enemy. They are only fighting our people while killing off their inner selves, their own Other. In this place of shadow, we the American people remain the enemy.

7

CULTURE AND "RACE"

What is culture?

What is culture? A second question could possibly develop, *whose culture*? This second inquiry is most valid and important in the ethnic mixture that America represents. In her opening discussion of culture in the essay "Theoretical and Conceptual Approaches to African and African American Psychology" author Linda James Meyers says:

> Our understanding of humanity is culture bound. Culture is the social force that informs our designs for living and patterns of interpreting reality. Thus, legitimate psychological study of humanity can be facilitated by giving appropriate regard to the cultural underpinnings informing our perceptions and shaping our interpretations as knowers. (p. 35)

The broad categories of defining culture include such random elements as dress, religion, food, art, and children rearing practices. In a discussion of specifically Africanist and collective American culture, the beginning definition of culture really does seem to require the second question as part of a necessary duality. The title of this book, *The Racial Complex*, seeks to explore culture and race from an Africanist Jungian perspective. I think about this perspective as including the individual ego of personhood, the personal unconscious with our complexes, and the collective unconscious as well as ancestors.

Our unconscious is expansive, deep, lovely and mostly incomprehensibly mysterious in all the ways that Jung has stated in his definition of the unconscious in *The Structure and Dynamics of the Psyche*:

> So defined, the unconscious depicts an extremely fluid state of affairs: everything of which I know but of which am not at the moment thinking; everything of which I was once conscious but have now forgotten; everything

perceived by my sense, but not noted by my conscious mind; everything which, involuntarily and without paying attention to it, I feel, think, remember, want, and do; all the future things that are taking shape in me and will sometime come to consciousness: all this is the content of the unconscious. (*Collected Works*, vol. 8, para 382)

I do believe this definition can in some ways be relational to our cultural selves. Are we not fluid as cultural individuals, as fluid as the cultural group to which we are members? In this moment I am thinking in a way that is defined by my cultural self—this self-created by circumstances, people and events in my current life as well as those of an ancestral lineage. Does not the self I am today hold who I will become in the future based on my cultural self? I believe there is fluidity in much of Jung's writings. This type of fluidity allows for what some have considered Jung's contradictions in his writings. I think that sometimes they are contradictions, paradoxes and at other times just moments of *flow*. This flow or fluidity can represent him as "a man of his times," while carrying the racial ethos of those times, and a man at the beginning path of pioneering a new and different modern psychology in Western healing practices.

A Jungian perspective on culture might take into account the psychological stance as viewed through the writing of Joseph Henderson, author of *Cultural Attitudes in Psychological Perspective* (1984). This text is considered to be the groundbreaking Jungian writing that addressed the presence of a cultural collective in 20th-century psychological thought.

This allows for a human presence in consciousness between the personal unconscious and the collective unconscious. It presents with a place of recognition for all that is cultural in the life. Henderson writes of four cultural attitudes: social, religious, aesthetic and philosophic. In defining the social attitude he states: "The social attitude, generally speaking, is concerned with maintaining the ethical code of the culture, whether of the established culture or any specific countercultural deviation from it" (p. 22). Henderson goes on to enlarge this point by indicating that the maintenance of a cultural code is possible as the individual through a process of relatedness to social events and human relationships grows in her own individuation process. He indicates that there is a balance to be achieved. Henderson says:

If one becomes too individualistic, the effect is psychic inflation and isolation from one's fellow men. If one lives too collectively, one becomes uncomfortably deflated and subtly depressed, though one's conformity may bring certain rewards. Individual morality is lowered to the collective norm in which one may find a xenophobic strength. This may become depressing, because its only justification is the soulless expediency of believing that if enough people hold the same beliefs or do the same things, they must all be right. If however, those values are proposed which embrace both individual and cultural needs, we have the condition necessary for individuation to appear in a social context. (p. 23)

Human beings are both individual and collective, have the sensibilities of both since both are required for the fullness of living. Henderson warns: "Therefore, one must avoid two dangers: that of too much individuality or of too much collectivity." I agree with him in the broad way of thinking about the cultural attitude as he has defined it but still wonder about the dismissal and critical negativity of the idea of *participation mystique* when referenced by Jungians and anthropologists and applied to Africans.

This might also be considered when thinking of clinical work with those of African diaspora since this theoretical idea of participation mystique can be one of the foundational pillars of Jungian psychological clinical work. The philosophical underpinnings of many African traditions and social systems are that the collective is of primary importance. It is of greater importance than the individual. This does not however negate the value of the individual in contributing to the collective. Each is valued or there could not exist a whole—a collective. The interruption of European projections into African philosophy took a recognized collective experience of Africans, created a phrase for it and a theoretical idea that was transformed into a negative *cultural* trait of reference for those undergoing Jungian psychology.

This is the definition of participation mystique found in *A Critical Dictionary of Jungian Analysis* (1986) by Andrew Samuels, Bani Shorter and Fred Plaut.

> Term borrowed from the anthropologist Levy-Bruhl. He used it to refer to a form of relationship with an object (meaning 'thing') in which the subject cannot distinguish himself from the thing. This rests on the notion, which may be prevalent in a *culture*, that the person/tribe and the thing—for instance a cult object or hold artifact—are already connected. When the state of participation mystique is entered, this connection comes to life. Jung used the term from 1912 onwards to refer to relationships between people in which the subject, or a part of him, attains an influence over the other, or vice versa ... Participation mystique or projective identification are early defences which also appear in adult pathology. (pp. 105–106)

In his discussion of participation mystique, in *Jung's Map of the Soul*, author Murray Stein in further defining Jung's use of the former term says: "There is an absence of awareness of a difference between oneself and one's perceptions on the one hand and the object in question on the other. To some extent, people stay in this state of participation mystique all their lives ... We are unconsciously united with the world around us." The belief is that this initial stage of consciousness, following Jung who theorized regarding five stages of consciousness, is the "lowest." (p. 179)

One of the main issues to be reconciled is the use of this term with its original identification with Africans. The European language—*participation mystique*, used to define aspects of the cultural life of African people in this circumstance, can be considered cultural appropriation. The term based on and taken from observation of the religious and communal practice of Africans—a part of their culture, was language later used in Jungian psychology as a descriptor for the *lowest* state of consciousness.

In our own 21st-century consciousness, I think we could begin to see the inappropriateness of such terminology usage. In writing of culture and race, this is an example of how the two have met at an intersection within the area of Jungian psychology that holds a negative connotation to Africans and their descendants. Lucien Levy-Bruhl wrote about African people as "primitive" and being of a primitive mind unlike whites who had a modern mind. In his book, *How Natives Think* (1910), the author expounded his theory of participation mystique showing the differences between Africans and whites and the intellectual "advancement" of consciousness (and intelligence) from a "primitive" mind to one that was not—European.

It might appear that it doesn't matter so much about what Levy-Bruhl thought, theoretically proposed or wrote about in 1910. We are one hundred years past that time. However, as we think and consider culture and my focus on Africanist culture intersecting with Jungian psychology, I feel it is necessary to highlight the past as well as present times because of the shadow and lack of visibility of change within the Jungian community regarding the "historical" past.

This past most oftentimes remains our present as participation mystique remains a tenet of teaching in Analytical Psychology. This is without any caveat or disclaimer to discuss the culturally racial inappropriateness of the term and its historical background.

In considering participation mystique as the lowest form of consciousness—the unconscious joining of individuals to others—how does this reconcile with the obvious cultural connection of Africanist people? It appears that in our clinical work as Jungian analysts or psychotherapists we must take a different view of how we have historically defined the work that we do, not only with individuals of Africanist descent, but everyone with whom we work. Is it applicable to any of us today to continue to use misappropriated terminology, derived from 19th-century negative racialized anthropology? Are we ready to accept that this remains with us today because we use language, and in many ways think that African culture as well as the philosophy that underpins it, is a "less" culture than that of Europeans? This became by extension a feature of the white American collective. In our lives today, with the political and social climate around the world, it is not a far reach or supposition to understand European thought of those early visitors who demeaned African culture to the racism that remains in American society today.

In the text *Confronting Cultural Trauma: Jungian Approaches to Understanding and Healing*, Jungian analyst author Astrid Berg (2014) in her essay "Engagement with the Other: Reflections from Post-Apartheid South Africa" says the following:

> Racism is endemic and unconscious; the fear we have of otherness is a deeply entrenched one … But it is not only in South Africa that racism plays a role; it is a human phenomenon that we resonate with those who belong "to us"' and either ignore the "other" or use the "other" as a repository for our unwanted thoughts and feelings. Otherness is detected most obviously in outer appearance. How we respond to outer differences in people is determined by our collective and personal complexes. In South Africa the collective complex is very much based on skin color, and this has become a part of most people's individual psyche. (p. 51)

This is not only true in South Africa but also in our American society. The difference is that it has taken us this very long time to recognize how deep is this entrenchment. Due to the length of time that we have engaged with the word *race* as a false-truth, an inappropriately applied linguistic concept and sociological terminology, we have within our individual unconscious psyches a dividing line based on differing ethnicities that is defined by "race." The inferiority of an "Other" has had great importance to maintaining the relevance of cultural differences based on racism. It becomes significant that "race," or ethnicity has acquired such significance in determining the value of culture. This is not only for whites but also certainly for blacks even when the former de-valued that of the latter.

The standard for creating a hierarchy of culture was established by white Europeans. We have lived with this standard for centuries. The idea of an established hierarchy of culture-value could only lead to division amongst different ethnic groups. The major problems—social, economic and psychological—is the ways Africanists have been oppressed, tortured and murdered into accepting the cultural belief system of the white hierarchy. Even further—why can't each culture have its own importance and worthiness based on the intrinsic value placed on it by the culture which is indigenous to that particular culture? The choosing of a model that places cultures in a hierarchy with those of color at the bottom has created innumerable problems for us as a *race* of people. We have different cultures that have evolved and changed through the centuries and yet we remain the same *race* of people.

The arrival of Europeans such as Christopher Columbus interrupted and began to systematically influence and destroy the culture of brown-skin people. This is not only an aspect of our historical past but also our present time reality, lived experiences. The following is from Linda James Meyers's essay "Theoretical and Conceptual Approaches to African and African American Psychology":

> As should be expected, each cultural group embraces its own perspectives and understanding of the world. The difficulty with embracing one's own cultural frame of reference lies for the most part in the prohibitions the perspective might hold against exploring and honoring the perspectives of other cultural groups. This difficulty mounts in accordance with the extent to which the other cultural group is one that has historically been perceived as inferior, exploited, dehumanized, and disenfranchised legally, socially, economically, educationally, and politically by the dominant cultural group. (Meyers, 2009, p. 36)

The ethnically diverse culture of all Americans has been without a doubt distorted and forever changed by the historical events of American slavery and American racism. This type of distortion has affected and impacted both positively and negatively on our cultural racial complexes that have developed in the unconscious by way of archetypal energies, cognitive science, as well as the acting out behaviors of racism that has come to be a part of our American lives. The creation of culture for all the ethnic groups in America is influenced by unconscious psychic material. Our environment adds recognizable features to our understanding of our culture.

The culture of Africanist people has and continues to evolve from an African consciousness that is present and relevant today. A number of approaches connected to racism meant to end African culture have not succeeded because a culture can change, will transform while holding survival within its core, holding to the archetypal DNA of its foundation. In writing of racial and cultural identity, author Thomas A. Parham, in "Foundations for an African American Foundation: Extending Roots to an Ancient Kemetic Past" in *Handbook of African Psychology*, referencing the difference between cultural and racial identity says:

> It is a cultural rather than a racial analysis that best illuminates the psychology of a people ... Race is not a biological construction but rather a social construction, used not only to categorize people by degrees of melanin content in their skin but also to stratify groups in some artificial social hierarchy that assigns worth, and access to opportunity and privilege, on the basis of skin color. (pp. 6–7)

Parham further says in more deeply defining culture:

> It is at the deep-structured level of culture where the psychology of a people can best be understood, referenced, and interpreted. It is culture that colors and shapes a people's design for living patterns for interpreting reality. It is culture that provides an axiological interpretation of a people's value system that sees the following: an integrated versus a fragmented vision of the self; feelings as a emotional tone that should be expressed, rather than suppressed; a survival orientation that is collective, as opposed to individualistic and competitive; a sense of time that is fluid, as opposed to linear; a relationship to the universe that is in harmony with, instead of control of; and a sense of worth is based on contribution to one's community, as opposed to the acquisition of material wealth and possessions. (p. 6)

Our ideas of culture are defined not only by observable conscious behaviors that we exhibit but also by the unconscious activities of our psyche. In my discussion of the racial complex, named by three others as a *color complex* (Adams, Lind, Berg), I view this complex as making demands upon us based on social and historical patterns occurring within and outside of conscious knowing. Jung's definition of the unconscious previously given supports our knowledge as human beings while showing our limitations. The definition also shows the possibilities of depthful insights beyond what the ego can think itself to attain. It is in this going beyond the limits of the ego that we can visit the unconscious material that we reside within and make changes that alters our lives into a more meaningful way of living.

Culture comes from a "deep-structure level" of the unconscious. I think this is true of the personal unconscious (even with its environmental features that trigger deeper energies transformed into behaviors), and well as our collective unconscious. We live and behave out of unconscious forces that actually define who we are most of the time rather than us through ego consciousness creating this definition.

As I think about culture and a definition of it I acknowledge that my ancestral history was in existence before the beginning of American slavery. I also acknowledge that this ancestral history can come through me in almost unrecognizable patterns of behavior if and when my ego is a poor observer in my own life. In addition, I know that I can "forget" myself—parts of myself that I do not wish to see because I am blinded by ego desires for comfort/materialism or blinded by complex constellations that in one moment I may barely recognize and in another moment of which I have no memory.

How can I grasp, keep within—guiding principles of a cultural history that appears "lost"? How do I confront the "racial memory" of a racial complex that is so evocative and prone to constellation because of the nature of its genocidal trauma? If my psychological self "knows" its cultural history what are the ways at my means for remembering and making use of this knowledge? It appears that an Africanist racial complex when causing psychic eruption and brings undesired material to light is not only trying to show what might be considered negative but can also be a guidepost to that which is necessary for the cultural enlightenment and development of the individual as well as the cultural group.

When Maya Angelou wrote "And Still I Rise," Langston Hughes wrote "The Negro Speaks of Rivers" and Amiri Baraka wrote "Three Modes of History and Culture," I imagine that they and the poets and griots before them, and since them, have felt the activation of a racial complex that spoke to the imagination of a deep Africanist culture. These are the written works of individuals who I believe have been awakened by something of the unconscious that also demands an awakening of ego consciousness. This joining of ego and unconscious shows itself in the energetic aliveness that can produce a creative narrative whether it is linguistic, visual or both, that contains the crystals of the imiginal. This expression takes hold of a form within consciousness and dresses itself in the culture of the creator—in this case an Africanist who returns us to the remembrance of ourselves. This is certainly my experience of Hughes's poem that ends with the timeless words, *I've known rivers: Ancient, dusky rivers. My soul has grown deep like the rivers.* (p. 73)

When I consider the racial complex from an African American perspective, I believe that there are structural, archetypal patterns in place that can reach back to before skin color was a major determinant of deciding cultural attributes.

However, I also believe that the archetypal influences of historical trauma placed on a people shapes who were are as a cultural group as well as who we became. The writings of the poets named above speak to historical trauma revisited by a racial complex and showing itself in the archetypal Self through creativity. This experience is not limited to writers but also includes painters, dancers, musicians—especially of Africanist music and musicians who carried the rhythms of Africa to the American shores—South and North.

How do we change the emphasis within an Africanist culture that has become defined by the African Holocaust? Are we able to initiate or consciously participate in such a change? Do we wish to walk away from such an archetypal event and because of its nature as archetypal is walking away possible?

What is racism?

The history of archetypal events has signified that there are certain patterns in our human nature that have not disappeared over centuries. One such pattern is the human relationship of master to slave, the subservient to the privileged. In our contemporary lives we recognize this circumstance as we see this archetypal pattern thrive in the sale of women and children as sex slaves.

> What is racism? The word has represented daily reality to millions of black people for centuries, yet it is rarely defined—perhaps just because that reality has been such a commonplace. By "racism" we mean the predication of decisions and policies on consideration of race for the purpose of subordinating a racial group and maintaining control over that group. (Stokely Carmichael, *Racism: Essential Readings*, p. 112)

This is not an imaginative state of affairs but a reality that once again duplicates a pattern of a group of human beings disempowered by a more moneyed and economically powerful group. When I discuss the racial complex as exhibiting such a pattern as master to slave, I am recalling this pattern as an aspect of the racial complex but not limited to it. Jung has said that complexes and archetypal energies coming from our unconscious selves control us—they have the power that our egos cannot possibly have without making a conscious effort. The consciousness of this effort I believe also involves the use of will. We must wish to have a different experience of the Other—one that is not limited to a need for power over or control of this Other. This has not happened so far in our 21st century.

The idea of race has been a most economic, dominant and forceful tool for extending white privilege through centuries. The most essential thread holding this is place was and continues to be the "creation" of an Other. This Other becomes all that is required by the privileged to determine "status" and maintain power. This power is psychological, social, economic and educational. This is the pattern recognized in all phases of American race relations.

Toni Morrison in *The Origin of Others* (2017) discusses her own personal experience of being stranger to another and to herself. She tells us of how one day she meets a woman, a stranger, with whom she engages in a lively conversation—one in which she appears to hope to have a future engagement—"I imagine a friendship, casual, effortless, delightful." (p. 32) The two women agree to meet the following day, however, the stranger does not appear and Morrison begins to have questions about her own need for the "fisherwoman," a woman who she begins to suspect is only a thief, poaching an absent neighbor's fish. She says:

> Why should we want to know a stranger when it is easier to estrange another? Why should we want to close the distance when we can close the gate … To understand that I was longing for and missing some aspect of myself. (p. 38)

The anticipation expressed by Morrison is not unlike the arousal we feel in want-ing to meet the stranger, the Other. However, I think that we always have the fear of meeting in a warm authenticity while pushing away from and this psychological push-pull is hard to endure. Oftentimes, within the clinical setting we see this kind of suffering within the patient, within our selves as analysts and within the trans-ference. We want intimacy with another and yet cannot bring ourselves to own our "mirrored" reflection that is projected onto an Other.

These projections within the context of the racial complex when directed at Africanist individuals or cultural groups and others of color, can contain the racist patterns of thinking that has enabled racism in our society for many centuries. In the Foreword to Morrison's book Ta-Nehisi Coates writes: "Racism matters. To be an Other in this country matters—and the disheartening truth is that it will likely continue to matter" (p. viii).

In the language of Jungian psychology these are the words that could define a psychological complex—any complex because they do matter, as well as a tradition that has been to have people of color be the Other. They have been the Other because of differences of skin color, language, "consciousness" cultural attributes and much more. They have held the cast-off white shadow projected onto them as part of the theoretical foundation of a Eurocentric psychology.

Author Lawrence W. Levine writes in *Black Culture and Black Consciousness: Afro-American Folk Thought from Slavery to Freedom* (2007), about the culture of African Americans within the context of folk stories, music and from "the orally trans-mitted expressive culture of Afro-Americans in the United States during the cen-tury that stretched from the antebellum era to the end of the 1940s ..." (p. xxiv). In his chapter "The Rise of Secular Song" he notes the following:

> On the subjects of race and culture, twentieth-century Negroes were surrounded by cultural and ideological confusion and ambiguity rivaling that which had pla-gued their slave forebears ... We have been led to believe that, in the midst of this ambiguity, blacks wanted nothing more than to be white. But even if everything in the culture around them had been conducive to creating this desire, the impossible wish itself ran directly counter to the realistic, practical thrust so prominent in black consciousness. (p. 291)

In this statement, I am able to recall a thought expressed by Jung as he spoke of African Americans and their desire to be white. This was he felt, an aspect of the "Negro" racial complex. Levine counters Jung's proposition with his statement regarding this "impossible wish" by the "practical" common sense that existed in black conscious-ness. Being black had its own power that ran through the lives of the group could not be extinguished through centuries of slavery or "wishful" theoretical projections.

The resiliency of slaves proved itself repeatedly as an archetypal energy that emerged in each generation. This energetic push was always included a pattern of archetypal freedom. The whiteness of the Other could represent for Africanist people one thing alone and that was freedom from the yoke of slavery which they represented. W.E. Du Bois says of the American Negro in the duality of being black and American:

> He would not Africanize America, for America has too much to teach the world and Africa. He would not bleach his Negro soul in a flood of white Americanism, for he knows that Negro blood has a message for the world. (*The Souls of Black Folks*)

The recognition of a racial complex that suggested Africanist people wished to be white and abandon their culture is grossly inaccurate and in itself appears racist. I believe that whatever imitative patterns of behavior we have adopted as a social group show our willingness to change in a way of circumstance and perhaps convenience to the times. I do believe that any individual of color who engages in this type of physical change for example, bleaching their skin is seeking to find a difference—to find their other selves. I do not believe an entire cultural group of people—millions—wish to become white. I think that our cultural racial complex demands much of us. It might demand that at its affect we feel jealousy, rage, a deep sadness and much more on an emotional level. Perhaps, the idea of our "desire" to be white is an aspect of a white imagination and its own racial complex constellated by a desire to reclaim all the racial *exotic* shadow projections that Africanist people have held as a group over the centuries. Is this really a white Other only wanting and desiring more of themselves? In their confusion, Africanist people become the ones who are desiring them—is it really only projection?

8

CULTURAL TRAUMA AND THE RACIAL COMPLEX

Cultural trauma

Cultural trauma as I write about it in this chapter is specific to the trauma of the Africanist cultural group who with their ancestors experienced the suffering and after-effects of the African Holocaust. The relationship between the group experience of trauma and the racial complex are tied together in ways that define individuals but also group identity contemporary life, as well as possibly serving as the teleos projector of the future. I say this based on what appears to be in the nature of one of the most dramatic aspect of this particular group. I say this because the nature of our complexes is that they do not go away. The harder we fight to get rid of them the more they become determined to remain with us.

I believe that the consistent adherence of the particular racial complex of Africanist people reflect the particular trauma of the group's culture as people of color. The historical trauma of slavery and its aftermath had everything to do with creating the identity of African Americans. Their enslavement was directly due to their ethnicity. Long after whites, first bonded as indentured servants, had served their time and become freed individuals, blacks remained shackled in slavery.

In fact, the movement was purposeful and gave white colonials the free labor that they realized they required for economic freedom from England. In *A Different Mirror: A History of Multicultural America*, author Ronald Takaki says:

> Though they had been "sold," the first Africans in Virginia probably were not slaves, persons reduced to property and required to work without wages for life. In 1619, Virginia had no law legalizing slavery. Like many English colonists, the Africans were sold as indentured servants, bound by contract to serve a master for four to seven years in order to replay the expense of their passage. (p. 52)

However, within the next 40 years the situation had changed and Africans who had worked and lived side by side with white English indentured servants for these decades, were no longer to be free.

> In 1661, the Virginia Assembly began to institutionalize slavery. To make it de jure. A law regarding the punishment of servants referred to "those Negroes who are incapable of making satisfaction by addition of time." In other words, they were required to serve for life. Eight years later, the Virginia legislature defined a slave as property, a part of the owner's "estate." (p. 56)

It took almost half a century for the socio-political movement of Africans to become "indentured" from several years to becoming enslaved for life. The particular cruelty was that this was not only for their lifetimes but all of their generations to follow. Today we speak of the *survivor* as someone who has managed to escape from a mentally or physically painful situation. I believe that every African American who lives today is a survivor because the initial traumatic event continues to ripple through the conscious and unconscious lives of this cultural group. There are some who would suggest that the event of slavery can and should perhaps be left behind. That it is no longer an event that requires our attention.

If this is true to some in our American society, I do not believe it to be so for those who work in the field of psychology—especially Jungian psychology. We appear to be just at the initial opening conversations and dialogue within this area of specialty regarding discussions of race, racism and cultural complexes. As an example, in *Confronting Cultural Trauma: Jungian Approaches to Understanding Healing* (2014) there is no mention of African American cultural trauma. Essays in the edited book reflect trauma stories from Georgia, Caucasus, Germany, Estonia, even Russia. Many of the voices who speak of intergenerational trauma are international. In purchasing this book I had hoped to find an essay or two that could tell of something of the African American intergenerational cultural trauma. To consider ways of reflecting through Jungian work possibilities for healing. The closest I found was by Astrid Berg in her essay on the "Other" in her writing on post-apartheid South Africa. When I say that every living black person is a survivor I mean in all the ways that can be imaged and one of the principal ways is through visibility as a group member. We understand that those survivors of the Jewish Holocaust and their descendants have pledged never to forget. A striking note towards African Americans was almost ambivalence about "remembering." In a post Civil War era it seemed that in the attempts at reconciliation between North and South blacks were given minimal support. This support would have been to help remember the cultural suffering that had been endured for centuries. Instead the politics of the times took precedent and blacks were being asked to forget about slavery—almost as if it was a coincidental occurrence, not one that had changed the life pattern of millions and caused millions of death.

Africanist people cannot yet forget. I don't know that there will ever be a time to put slavery and its aftermath aside as an historical cultural event to be forgotten. In another of the essays from *Confronting Cultural Trauma*, author John Hill (2014) says:

> I consider the term *cultural trauma* as applying not only to the traumatization of an individual or group when cultural heritage is threatened, devalued, violated, scapegoated, or not allowed to take root and develop. I extend the meaning of cultural trauma to include certain behavior patterns, practices, assumptions, norms, and traditions that can induce trauma within one's own culture. (p. 32)

The trauma that occurs to an individual or group is inflicted from outside the group but can also be repeated over and again amongst family members. Author Hill addresses the issue through two case narratives how clinical work must engage differently than the usual "cultural habits" display in the family: "This is perhaps the reason resolution of the potentially deadly mix required an alternative cultural horizon, one that transcends the narrow confines of the parental home." (p. 33)

I do not believe that anyone, even members within the cultural group can say when an impactful event such as a cultural holocaust and its emotionally traumatizing conditions must end. I do believe that there are natural life rhythms. It does not feel that we are at the end of a cycle that addresses releasing all of the trauma of this cultural event. A major problem with seeking the "ending" and closure to all the cultural artifacts of American slavery is that we are now only beginning to really see them.

As we see the cultural parts of ourselves exposed and displayed to one another within our cultural group as well as others, after centuries, it allows us to see and understand more of who we are in this 21st century. We are formed and shaped by our past. It continues to influence us today. My own belief in allowing for the transcendence of something greater that can hold the cultural energy of my ancestral group, supports me in thinking that we must embrace all that has happened to us—to not forget, so that we can learn psychological and social lessons that may be hard to endure seeing. I think we are only beginning to really see the horror of what transpired with Africanist people. *Black Rage*, by William H. Grier and Price M. Cobbs, first written in 1968 during a time of intense racial political, social and cultural eruptions, were addressing a racial environment that even today holds to certain patterns. The authors say:

> To be "colored" has meant far more than riding in the back of the bus. To be sure, there is great misery in being the last hired and first fired and relegated to decaying sections of town, but there is enduring grief in being made to feel inferior. (p. 30)

I do believe that as a cultural group we continue to endure.

Since the writing of *Black Rage*, certainly some events have occurred that seems to have pushed us forward towards a more humanizing view of the cultural group. However, the internal self-view that has a personal unconscious must also change. The ego must become unafraid.

> To be a bondsman was to experience a psychological development very different from the master's. Slavery required the creation of a particular kind of person, one compatible with a life of involuntary servitude. The ideal slave

had to be absolutely dependent and have a deep consciousness of personal inferiority. His color was made the badge of that degradation. And as a final precaution, he was instilled with a sense of the unlimited power of his master. Teachings so painstakingly applied do not disappear easily. (p. 26)

Privilege, Power and Difference (2017) is in its third edition of publication. The author Allan G. Johnson relates a story of being at dinner with a colleague. Here is what he says. Compare it to authors Cobbs and Grier in the above quote:

The simple truth is that when I go shopping, I'll probably get waited on faster and better than she will (a female black colleague). I'll benefit from the *cultural assumption* that I'm a serious customer who doesn't need to be followed around to keep me from stealing something. The clerk won't ask for three kinds of ID before accepting my check or accepting my credit card. But all these indignities that my whiteness protects me from are part of her everyday existence. And it doesn't matter how she dresses or behaves or that she's an executive in a large corporation. Her being black and the realtors' and bankers' and clerks' being white in a racist society is all it takes. (p. 6)

The first passage above written by two black psychiatrists 50 years ago addresses the real life experiences of a black person today as seen through the eyes of a white male. In our time we can speak of cultural assumptions—Johnson does with a casualness that addresses our having become accustomed to seeing and realizing cultural differences and cultural discrimination. As a woman of an Africanist cultural group I have been followed in a store due to a *white cultural understanding* that I may be a shoplifter. The constellation of my racial complex heats emotionally first in anger. Then comes a typical reaction when something deep is activated moving into conscious awareness—some confusion, should I say something or just keep shopping? This is not a made-up story. This is my lived experience as a black woman. When I left my home before even getting into the car to drive to the store I have a *black cultural understanding*.

I may be suspected of stealing.

There is enduring grief in being made to feel inferior.

Authors Grier and Cobbs write about the emotional state that American black men must endure. They have defined these states within the context of black culture. In speaking of survival as a black man, the authors say:

He must cushion himself against cheating, slander, humiliation, and outright mistreatment by the official representatives of society … For his own survival, then, he must develop a *cultural paranoia* in which every white man is a potential enemy unless proved otherwise and every social system is set against him unless he personally finds out differently. (p. 178)

In their discussion of what they have defined as "The Black Norm," authors Grier and Cobbs reinforce the importance of psychology clinicians recognizing what they have called "character traits" for success and survival in the society. I do not think these "norms" have changed that drastically since the writing of their book. The authors have spoken of a *cultural depression, cultural masochism and cultural anti-socialism*—all necessary to living as a black man (p. 178). The experience of living is a way that allows for maintaining the best psychological health that one can under the circumstances of insidious racism.

The cultural paranoia of which the co-authors write is a necessary condition of being black. I also believe it adds a particular stress to the lives of those who live within this Africanist cultural group. Group survival has endured over the centuries because there have been mental adjustments and behaviors developed in service of survival.

Cultural artifacts have been lost and replaced by perhaps more necessary ones dealing with psychological presence of mind.

> The culture of slavery was never undone for either master or slave. The civilization that tolerated slavery dropped its slaveholding cloak but the inner feelings remained. The "peculiar institution" continues to exert its evil influence over the nation. The practice of slavery stopped over a hundred years ago, but the minds of our citizens have never been freed. (*Black Rage*, p. 26)

How do we free our minds? I think this has been a struggle of the American collective since before the Emancipation Proclamation. Even in the 1700s before and after the American Revolution, the call for freedom of all men was being heard in various parts of the world. I suggest that we have such difficulty with freeing our minds because we might be too dependent on thinking of this freedom as coming only from the center of ego consciousness. When we consider the possibility of being bound to an archetypal pattern of master-slave, we must recognize that the ego alone does not have control over such an archetypal energy that has dominated human consciousness since biblical times.

Can we consider freeing our minds because we search inside ourselves in a deeper place that does connect to our personal unconscious? Can we consider gaining more freedom of consciousness by thinking of racial complexes and the force they exhibit upon us while we continue to engage in separating from an Other who really is perhaps different by culture yet kin in many other ways?

In *My Grandmother's Hands: Racialized Trauma and the Pathway to mending Our Hearts and Bodies* (2017), by Resmaa Menakem, the author's focus is on how we can truly live in our bodies through understanding what he identifies as racialized trauma. I agree with Menakem when he says the following:

> For the past three decades, we've earnestly tried to address white-body supremacy in America with reason, principles, and ideas—using dialogue, forms,

discussion, education, and mental training. But the widespread destruction of Black bodies continues.

And some of the ugliest destruction originates with our police. Why is there such a chasm between our well-intentioned attempts to heal and the ever-growing number of dark-skinned bodies who are killed or inured, sometimes by police officers? … Our bodies have a form of knowledge that is different from our cognitive brains. This knowledge is typically experienced as a felt sense of constriction or expansion, pain or ease, energy or numbness. Often this knowledge is stored in our bodies as wordless stories about what is safe and what is dangerous. The body is where fear, hope, and react; where we constrict and release; and where we reflexively fight, flee, or freeze. If we are to upend the status quo of white-body supremacy, we must begin with our bodies. (pp. 4–5)

It seems that there still needs to be a pairing of our bodies as well as that part of ourselves that comes from our unconscious selves. Author Menakem goes on to discuss neuroscience and its vagus nerve and his substitution of the words *soul nerve*, to explain this connector between our primal brain's instinctive focus on survival. Menakem says, "trauma is not primarily an emotional response. Trauma always happens in the body" (p. 7).

The re-occurring trauma that happens on a bodily level is a memory and a physical reminder of something that has happened before that was painful. It is an aspect of our human survival that allows us to continue protecting ourselves. However, the "protection" that we have offered to ourselves within our cultural groups both white and black has worked to create antagonisms bound by a racial complex which functions as part of our unique cultural complexes.

Samuel Kimbles in *Phantom Narratives: The Unseen Contributions of Culture to Psyche* (2014) provides his definition of cultural complexes. He says,

I have identified five basic elements five basic elements … (1) they function at the group level of the individual psyche and within the group; (2) they function autonomously; (3) they organize group life; (4) they facilitate the individual's relationship to the group; and (5) they provide a sense of belonging and identity as well as a sense of historical continuity. (p. 83)

As part of the Antioch University gathering that I spoke of earlier in Chapter 3 of this book, I had my own countertransference experience to much of the material discussed that day. Something that became clearer to me was my own reluctance to work more with culturally white racial complex material as part of audience discussions. This was confirmed a few weeks later as I provided a lecture at a psychoanalytical institute. Someone from the audience wanted to know why I didn't say more about the white culture racial complex. I have thought about this question more since these two most recent events. One reason is that I believe we—the Africanist people cultural group, have much history of our own that requires revisiting. This revisiting can be demanding because of the nature of the loss that we experienced through the centuries. My curiosity and endurance for exploring our cultural richness draws my attention. I am also curious regarding a white cultural complex that engages with racism but mostly in so much as it affects my cultural group or in an intentional, planned exchange where whites are invested in investigating and discussing their white racial complex. I find the absence still of strong and viable voices of color within the field of psychology—literature, training programs and clinical settings, all sufficient reasons to focus on speaking from a space of the Africanist culture.

Samuel Kimbles in his own writing relates the personal aspect of how he came to choose his specific work on cultural complexes. At first he relates a dream he had the night before his interview to gain entry to the Jungian analytical candidate training program. In this dream he meets with several black men who insist that he join with them in giving a "secret handshake" before parting ways.

Kimbles says:

> Because the Jungian tradition has tended to regard cultural and group processes as exogamous to the individual's development, the significance of culture for individuation has often been overlook. According to the promise I gave the other black men in this dream, my personal and clinical development en route to analytic training would have to be different. I would have to recognize that working with cultural issues was intimately related to individuation ... Kinship and loyalty issues, power dynamics, oppression, and guilt could, therefore, remain within my mind as a context for analytic training. (p. 5)

In a similar way I have found the need for a deepening of my own consciousness through my work with others that is inclusive of my own cultural heritage, psychoanalytical processes and racial healing. I entered into Jungian studies via dreamwork. This and the obvious need to develop more knowledge regarding our cultural psychological processes regarding outstanding social issues such as racism has called to me. I have previously discussed much of this in the Introduction chapter of this book and a previous publication (Brewster, 2017).

The presence of ethnicity in Jungian psychology as a practice and an area of general psychology is evolving. In his classic text, *Complex: Diagnosis and Therapy in Analytical Psychology* (1999), Hans Dieckmann addresses the Oedipus Complex.

He describes the myth and applies his own interpretation. Important to note is his reference to what might perhaps be a misuse of this myth in regards to non-white cultures:

> The Oedipus complex is not valid for all cultures, but rather specific to our culture. Stein (1974) has pointed out that there are many primal peoples who do not have an incest taboo vis a vis the parents but only in regard to siblings. We can no longer denigrate this as something primitive and preoedipal, as was done in the nineteenth and early twentieth centuries; rather, we know today,

thanks to extensive ethnological studies, that the so-called primitive peoples were not at all primitive but had developed areas other than natural science and technology. In these areas they were just as differentiated and, in part, superior to us, as Levi-Strauss (1966) has shown. (p. 112)

Cultural group differences should not make us abnormal, wicked or abhorrent to one another. However, because of our very long history of the intrusive invention of race and racism into our cultural experiences, we have increased our possibilities for being at opposites and creating an Other. Jung's theory of the Opposites I do believe is relevant to our discussion of the racial complex because whether we believe it or not, on an unconscious level it supports us as being in a struggle of separation. In *Collected Works*, volume 14, Jung says: "The opposites are the ineradicable and indispensable preconditions of all psychic life" (para 206). In expanding this idea Jung believed that the pull of opposites on an energetic level took place within the individual, between couples and between groups. In the distancing that can happen between oneself and the Stranger, the Other as previously discussed by Toni Morrison, we see it on the individual level. In times of warfare and racial strife we see it within our cultural groups.

Jung's idea of the naturalness of seeing the Other as separate and perhaps cautiously is perhaps for the ego's understanding of safety and survival. One of the more recent publicized theories of neuroscience is that we have a biological transmission in our brains that become activated when we see someone who is different from us. Our positive reaction to them is lessened than if we see someone who is similar—as in skin color. This has become a most immediate identifier of difference in our American society. It is also not only an indicator of ethnic difference but also can have with it many negative unconscious and conscious connotations. This would influence the length before there can be a positive response time (if any), within the encounter of one another.

Opposites in the complex

I return now to the discussion of racial complexes, which I view as a very significant strand in the psychic tapestry of the larger cultural complex. The ability of Africanist people to cope with cultural trauma over many centuries can occur because of resiliency and is tied directly to Jung's theory of Opposites and the functional shift of compensatory action that takes place on an unconscious level. The magnitude of slavery, civil war, Jim Crow, all added to a group collective complex activation over decades. On an unconscious level with slavery in place, the archetypal energy of Africanist freedom was also seeking and was expressed through the efforts of many individuals and groups. The compensatory activation of cultural complexes resulted in the Civil War, the reactionary events of Jim Crow following the war and a few decades later grew into the fullness of the Civil Rights Movement. In our primal selves we want to be safe. Our ego wants this in addition to comfort and all the privileges that life can afford.

The push-pull of unconscious racial complexes traumatized by centuries of physical pain, emotional torture and psychological suffering, including the deaths of hundreds of thousands, lived /lives in the body as well as in the group consciousness of Africanist people.

Carol Anderson, author of *White Rage: The Unspoken Truth of Our Racial Divide* (2016), says what I perceive of as an example of the working of Jung's Opposites in discussing the white rage of what I identify as a white cultural complex:

> White rage is not about visible violence, but rather it works its way through the courts, the legislatures, and a range of government bureaucracies ... It is not the mere presence of black people that is the problem ... It is blackness that refuses to accept subjugation, to give up. (pp. 4–5)

Blackness that refuses to give up is the oppositional energy force that confronts a white racial complex within a group dynamic that slithers through the "halls of power." The socially activated group Africanist complex that is charged by an archetypal force, *always* directed to freedom, is too much to be met directly head on with the exception of the Klan, and a few other white nationalist organizations. However, what we see, as Anderson has pointed out, is the erosion of Africanist gains—fought by way of blood, death and the centuries of loss. White rage, as part of a cultural racial complex expressing itself behaviorally happened in Charlottesville as the last major and most recent incident of this type of expression. As I watch the appointment of Kavenaugh to the Supreme Court and other Federal Court justices, I recognize a packing of the courts that is for the sole purpose of denying people of color their civil liberties. African Americans have learned that even with the force of judicial strength through laws, our racial trauma and cultural collective always remains in a state of cultural paranoia. In our individual stance as part of this cultural group our sense of a lack of safety—politically, socially and economically, will not let us rest—not for long. This is the opposite of white privilege that does not need such an awareness of the need for safety in these areas.

Racial complexes, like our trauma, can be subtle or visible.

Like a burning forest fire or a yet undetected fever in the body. This is not unlike the fires of dissent we experienced in the 1960s and 1970s. The connection between our Africanist racial complexes and our cultural trauma are so intertwined that I do not believe we will ever be able to separate the two. They were born together out of the white racial consciousness of greed, power and the archetypal demand of expression for a master—slave relationship. The cultural expression of this archetype took its form in American slavery. Complexes are subtle, and we are caught in them more often than we are aware. It is generally in hindsight that we can see them. Within our cultural groups, we can gain more knowledge about being caught in a cultural complex. Our black cultural racial complexes I believe have protected us from extinction. Millions of us died—without anyone to mourn for us. Still we survived. This is the powerful insistence of collective memory that can gather strength from a tragic history that will not be forgotten. It is essential that this past not be forgotten. I think it must be remembered and incorporated into the vision of what is still necessary and essential for the transcendence—a consistent re-emerging of a third energy coming from the tension of cultural group opposites.

If there are psychic opposites operating within us as individuals and as members of cultural groups and these opposites can show themselves from the negative spectrum of the racial complex, how do we find our way in consciousness to the positive end with greater frequency? We know our trauma. We are continuously learning about our psychological racial unconsciousness selves. What is the flow of learning—as a transcendent symbol, a living reality that can emerge to support healing our bodies and spirit of racism and cultural trauma?

9

TRANSFERENCE AND COUNTERTRANSFERENCE

The art and craft of Jungian psychological work includes the recognition of what transpires between analyst and analysand in what is commonly known as the *transference*. Jungian psychology has gradually grown to be a pillar that supports this concept first named by Freud and later adopted by Jung in his Analytical Psychology. It was a discussion of the transference as the "alpha and omega" of psychotherapy that first brought high interest to both Freud and Jung at their initial meeting in 1907. Jung understood and promoted the transference as vitally important to the exchanges that happen between therapist and client each time they are engaged with one another. Even as he stressed the importance of the transference, Jung says the following in *Collected Works*, vol. 16, paragraph 359 regarding the transference:

> I personally am always glad when there is only a mild transference or when it is practically unnoticeable. Far less claim is then made upon one as a person, and one can be satisfied with other therapeutically effective factors. Among these the patient's own insight play an important part, also his goodwill, the doctor's authority, suggestion, good advice, understanding, sympathy, encouragement, etc. Naturally the more serious cases do not come into this category.

As I read Jung's words I think about the more relational aspect of sitting with a client. Understanding, empathy and all that he says comes into the experience of being with one another. However, as I experience the transference and counter-transference there is much more and Jung does address this in various places in his essays in *The Psychology of the Transference*.

It is significant that Jung also previously stated that the transference was a hindrance to a patient obtaining a healing from the psychological work. (*CW* 16, para 349). Though Jung expressed a variety of ideas about the transference, I believe that he always considered it to be relevant to clinical work. Those Jungian practitioners who have followed

Jung, though changing the conceptualization of the transference, continue to understand its significance to the implementation of clinical Jungian psychology.

Jung in his eventual publication of *The Psychology of the Transference* decided to use alchemy and its picture symbols of the Rosarium philosophorum to express his theory of the transference within the clinical setting. He speaks of the relationship of two people, their projections and the reclaiming of their unconscious material:

> Practice analysis has shown that unconscious contents are invariably projected at first upon concrete persons and situations. Many projections can ultimately be integrated back into the individual once he has recognized their subjective origin; others resist integration, and although they may be detached from their original objects, they thereupon transfer themselves to the doctor. (*CW* 16, para 357)

Jung further states: "This bond is often of such intensity that we could almost speak of a "combination." When two chemical substances combine, both are altered" (para 358). This idea of a combination resulted in Jung using the word *coniunctio* to represent how psychotherapist and client become one through the transference.

The connection that occurs between patient and analyst can be uncomfortable. Jung says that in the clinical work due to the activation of unconscious complexes and archetypal energies, the patient can lose touch with ego's personality:

> It is like passing through the valley of the shadow, and sometimes the patient has to cling to the doctor as the last remaining shred of reality. This situation is difficult and distressing for both parties; often the doctor is in much the same position as the alchemist who no longer knew whether he was melting the mysterious amalgam in the crucible or whether he was the salamander glowing in the fire. (para 399)

In this fire of the developing relationship, Jung says both patient and analyst are transformed by the work. The latter is held to "go to the limits of his subjective possibilities" (*CW* vol. 16, para 400). The revealing of vulnerabilities and exposure to the true suffering which brought the patient into the temenos and which the analyst share reveals:

> No longer the earlier ego with its make-believes and artificial contrivances, but another, "objective" ego, which for tis reason is better called the "self." No longer a mere selection of suitable fictions, but a string of hard facts, which together make up the cross we all have to carry or the fate we ourselves are. (*CW* vol. 16, para 400)

Jung's words hold the potency of the metaphorical and authentic sway of the transference within the clinical setting. A major goal of psychological work that includes the transference is for the client and the therapist to be touched and changed by the work due to conscious as well as unconscious talk, empathy and broadened engagement. The joining of two in the alchemical represents the joining of therapist and patient in the clinical work. Within this joining, the transference occurs and hopefully something is achieved which addresses exposure of the psychological selves to one another.

As a result, the patient as well as the therapist changes.

Leslie C. Jackson and Beverly Greene, editors of *Psychotherapy with African American Women: Innovations in Psychodynamic Perspectives and Practice*, offer essays by a number of clinicians. One such essay, "The Interweaving of Cultural and Intrapsychic Issues in the Therapeutic Relationship" addresses what authors Kumea Shorter-Gooden and Leslie C. Jackson define as the *cultural transference*. They state:

> We define cultural transference even more broadly as the emotional reactions of a client to the therapist based on the client's sense of who the therapist is culturally with respect to race, ethnicity, religion, gender, age, social class, and other factors … The cultural transference and how it is acknowledged and dealt with is an important element in forming the therapeutic alliance. (p. 20)

It is important for therapists of color to recognize not only the psychological problems that we encounter but also the importance of being with one another in the healing of these problems. Since the beginning of psychological services being available to American patients, African Americans have been discriminated against in the delivery of these services. This was due to the natural bias against African Americans that is an aspect of institutional racism including the belief that blacks did not require any "additional" attention other than minimal medical care. This is a part of a false paradoxical mythology that holds Africanist people as inferior and yet unworthy of needing any or much good care while being an economic measurement of white success. In fact, the early medical treatments that were mostly directed at black women in their child-bearing years for the benefit of the plantation system and later the labor market. Healthcare was generally given within a cultural context—natural healers and medicine women.

In their discussion of projection, the authors state:

> One of the challenges in the African American female client-African American female therapist dyad is that how the client feels about herself may be immediately projected onto the therapist. If the client, for example, has negative feelings about being Black and female, these feelings may be thrust onto the therapist through the process of projection or of projective identification. (p. 22)

Every patient of Africanist ancestry that has come to me for psychological support in deepening herself with the exception of one has expressed a positive, sometimes idealized aspect of the transference. I welcome this type of transference. I also believe that a negative mother complex must at some point become activated so that whatever is holding the patient captive will allow her to be released through the work done on the mother complex. I welcome the projections as a part of the natural course of our clinical work together. Nothing is forbidden or negated in the transferential experience except those things that violate ethical boundaries.

The Shorter-Gooden and Jackson say: "Premature termination is often a problem when cultural transference is not attended to." I do believe I have experienced this as a clinician working with black patients. As the authors suggest there is not sufficient understanding and addressing, acknowledging where though we are of the same culture, we may have different backgrounds that keep us from meeting in the therapeutic alliance. I have found this to be true and sometimes go to my later recognition or guessing of my "therapist failure" to make a good enough attachment with the patient through a lack of sharing.

This might also be caused by my psychoanalytical "style" that is actually too "cool," insufficiently warm enough to bond on a cultural level. I have found that if this does not happen on a cultural level as a part of the transference, the therapy will more than likely be terminated sooner rather than later and leave me with a sense of my failure in the work and the incompleteness of it. I think there can still a certain amount of awkwardness that can be present even between two therapists of the same color. Our cultural transference can actually make it difficult to relate in terms of the therapeutic alliance because of unrealized expectations that are difficult to work through within the session.

Shorter-Gooden and Jackson write about the "Real Relationship" in following R. Greenson from *The Technique and Practice of Psychoanalysis* (1967). The authors say:

> Cultural transference and cultural countertransference attitudes are brought by the client and therapist into the therapeutic encounter and may not have anything to do with the reality of the particular clinician or client seated in the room. However, the real relationship between the pair is another important element that can facilitate or get in the way of the development of a therapeutic alliance. The real relationship is defined by Greenson (1967) as parts of the relationship between the therapist and the client that are realistic, in words, not inappropriate or fantasized, and genuine. (p. 26)

In my own work with patients there is room for a "real relationship" that includes a realism that takes in all that presents. The experience of somatic cues, discomforts in the body, fantasies, that which appears inappropriate to the ego, images, all become necessary aspects of the psychological work that is being done. This allows for the patient to have an imaginative experience within the room that is not ego bound and deals directly with unconscious material that may enter the phenomenological field.

Much of the work is based on permitting many different kinds of realities to enter. One of these realities points also to why I have become an analyst. How has my own cultural racial complex prompted and supported me with archetypal influences to spend time working within psychic space? How is this a factor?

M. J. Maher in her book *Racism and Cultural Diversity* (2012), says that in her own work as a clinician within groups she found it necessary to allow for ethnic differences to remain while accepting the egoic differences that could be present even amongst black clinicians. Maher says:

It is important that the individual, if possible, is allowed to work at their own pace of integration. Therefore, the decision to talk about racial issues should be guided by the readiness of the individual and the group, but sometimes that decision is taken away by unconscious processes such as transference and countertransference evoked in the here and now. The aim needs to be about understanding why what is happening at that particular moment. For example, if I walk into a room full of White women I might immediately be aware that we are all women (inclusive, defence against being alone) or I might become aware of being the only Black person (excluding, defence against being enmeshed, fear of losing one's identify, wanting to feel special). The work is in trying to understand why one reacts in one way and not the other at that particular moment, because that would give an understanding of the fears of feelings which influence one's reaction. (p. 143)

The cultural countertransference according to authors Shorter-Gooden and Jackson includes "the therapist's emotional reactions to the client based on the client's race, ethnicity, religion, gender, age social class or the like" (p. 24). These are certainly elements that enter into conscious awareness of the client. As I sit with clients I'm also trying to be aware of all the unconscious material that is entering the field. This unconscious material hopefully makes its way into ego awareness as I can experience it as a most important part of the countertransference.

Issues that present in the clinical work that have to do with my countertransference require careful inspection on my part. I have found over the years it is very important to notice my dreams when working with patients over issues where I feel tension in the work—when it is feeling de-railed in some way—as if something is off-center. This is good to notice in the work and helpful to providing perhaps a new, needed direction. Over time I have come to depend on the dreams to help point me in the "right" direction that psyche indicates it is time to move towards. I trust that dreams because of their connection with the unconscious are capable of giving me guidance always in conjunction with ego work. I cannot rely only on my ego in doing the work. The countertransference within the clinical work therefore includes dream work, somatic intentions, the "real relationship," emotions and much more. Nothing is excluded in my openness of perception as to what I am able to be willing to allow into my consciousness. This is my intention for all that happens in the transference as well as the countertransference.

I think it takes time to learn how to trust what may or may not appear in the field as part of the transference. In the case of a cultural transference what I hear happening most often from white therapist who work with black clients is that the former are afraid of "saying the wrong thing." I'm not certain that there is a "wrong thing." The issues discussed between myself and Africanist patients who have seen white therapists is that there is an experience of discomfort (in the field, in the body), that signifies not really being seen or heard by the white therapists. If the clinician cannot address an ethnically related issue with the client then the client will feel invisible. This I believe goes directly to a cultural issue experienced by Africanist people in a collective that has historically made them invisible except to be of service.

Africanist clients bring with them a historical past that includes not only the "typical" issues of unhappiness that brings one to therapy but also the collective racial issues that continuously add to their trauma. I do not believe we can provide psychotherapy for Africanist clients without acknowledging the effects of the African Holocaust. I do believe that this is a part of the real relationship that must occur at some point with the client. They will generally bring it up as part of the work due to the problem of insidious racism that we experience in our lives today. This racism is persistent, does not let up and as a part of the racial complex it represents on an unconscious level, always returns. Jung says that this return can be stronger than when originally experienced. Therefore clients of color will be engaged in clinical work oftentimes with expressed or unexpressed/unidentified ideas that have to do with their racial complexes. Most times, it is essential to work with these patients in helping them identify their cultural racial complexes so that they can learn how to release themselves from feelings of guilt, depression and anger.

I am not saying that these are "bad" states of attention or unworthy of being experienced. I am proposing that the cultural awareness of why a particular guilt complex is being activated must be recognized. For example, the mother who is weary from working two jobs with the support of her own mother who helps her may feel guilt for not being there for enough time with her children. It is natural that the extended nature of black families allows for the grandmother to become primary caretaker. This still does not alleviate the guilt feelings of the mother.

I have found in the clinical work that these feelings of guilt tied to this complex in Africanist women, can be almost archetypal in nature. They become insistent on working harder, never taking breaks and feeling all the intense anxiety of overburdening themselves. I think this is a part of our cultural trauma that holds the collective memory of belonging to another where there was "no rest for the weary." These might also be Africanist women who drive themselves even after material success has been accomplished. There is an inability to enjoy what they have earned. There is an inability to emotionally feel empowerment or the joy of entitlement due to achievement.

What keeps us from claiming what rightfully belongs to us after the struggle? Are we too afraid that it will be taken away from us in some way—that we cannot own anything? Nothing can belong to us? Is this a part of the racial complex as the young African American woman spoke of at Antioch? Is this a key issue of how we "survive" on an unconscious level—not taking what we have earned, not recognizing our privilege, not accepting all of the historical cultural suffering and seeing how we deserve all the goodness that comes our way?

This is certainly not all of who we are but I do think it is an aspect of our cultural unconscious selves. In the cultural racial complex within the context of only a Eurocentric psychological model, Africanist people can come to stand in the middle of themselves as a group of black people who have developed from the black American experience.

Even when we may forget this for a moment, I believe something inside of us wakes us up and provides guidance in recognition of a Self that can identify true inner value.

White and Parham in *The Psychology of Blacks* state: "The remnants of the African tradition within black culture were handed down from generation to "generation by the oral tradition operating with informal and formal communal institutions such as the black church, extended family networks, fraternal orders, women's clubs, and street corner society" (p. 18).

How can these centuries of reflective bonding within our cultural group best be valued, respected and used in the clinical work of the cultural transference?

10

EMERGENCE FROM GRIEVANCE TO GRIEF: THE LITERARY ARTS

Journey as immigrant—journey as slave

The movement from grievance to grief is a journey. It is one that has many possibilities for failure as well as success. Even the goals of the journey may well change. The individuals and collective groups we meet on the journey can become our strongest allies as well as our most hated enemies. In the course of the journey we bring with us all that is our culture. This culture includes our language, music, dance, religion and our words—our language. This language of course includes our poems, the poetic-mythological traditions that have caused us to survive, love and have great hope in the face of great despair.

We step first now onto the path of travel, of immigration. The movement from one place to another with the hope for positive change. Changing a life, changing many lives, and of all the descendants to come. The journey of the African diaspora will be discussed not as immigration—because it was not, but rather as forced enslavement.

Today, more than 2,000 of our brown children are separated from their parents due to racist immigration politics.

Today our children of color are sitting and sleeping in cages.

Today our children of color are crying for their mothers and their fathers.

Jung writes of emerging as a possible place of opposition. I believe it can be that place where we are determined and committed to oppose that which is against our values, our morality and our integrity. The emergence of African American cultural literary thought and writings have grown from the seeds of opposition spread upon the Earth since the beginning days of American slavery. My own writing follows in the tradition of others before me who write not only in opposition but also in grievance.

When I first began preparing this chapter I had hoped to spend a good amount of time speaking about the emergence of grievance and grief without too much of a focus on the political. I think I still can elicit these two states of attention but it is more difficult than I had imaged it would be because the weight of grievance sits more heavy now because of recent events—attacks on our women's rights, civil rights and personal citizen liberties.

Grievance wants to have a louder voice than grief because I think the frustration of an archetypal anger once again burst forth. I think that the pain of seeing children captured and taken from their parents causes our blood to get hot.

The journey of grievance to grief is bloody. As Americans we have engaged in shedding the blood of many ancestors. My own ancestral line began on the West coast of Africa and from there onto the slave auction blocks in Charleston, South Carolina. I cannot know how many of my ancestors bled to death on the Middle Passage journey, experienced the hot blood of fever, or how many died on the rice plantations of South Carolina. Shedding their blood under the whip. This plantation enslavement would have lasted for over a century.

Jung in writing about emergence acknowledges that we are oftentimes looking backwards, over our shoulders, as we struggle to birth something, to have it emerge in contemporary times. The journey from grievance to grief is a story of psychological trauma and the struggle to birth transformation from slavery to freedom. For those of Africanist descent, this story is yet to be told in its fullness. We are at the very beginning stages of telling the story of American slavery. This is an emerging narrative that joins in meeting its own historical reflection in our 21st-century lives. It is echoed in the voices of people of color—families as they once again endure the cultural trauma of separation from their kin against a movement that is purely an expression of racism. Colored people from Central and South America approach our borders hoping for change, for freedom. They are met at the border with racism. Their families have been separated and they have been imprisoned and caged.

Americans are seeing the emergence of the face of the collective cultural complex of racism that has not shown itself so broadly and forcefully since the reaction to Dr. Martin Luther King's protest marches that began at the end of the 1950s. This is who we were. This is who we are—as Americans and as collective witnesses.

When Carl Jung returned to America in 1937 for the Terry Lectures at Yale, the Tuskegee Study had been in progress for five years. In 1930, Jung wrote a paper that was first entitled, "Your Negroid and Indian Behavior" with a later change of title to "The Complications of American Psychology" when published as part of the *Collected Works*. (*CW* vol. 10, paras 946–980).

In this paper, Jung goes into detail stating his views on African Americans, and their relationship with white Americans, noting all of the negative possibilities for whites because of the "primitive" influences by African Americans:

> The white man is a most terrific problem to the Negro, and whenever you affect somebody so profoundly, then, in a mysterious way, something comes back from him to yourself. The Negro by his mere presence is a source of temperamental and mimetic infection, which the European can't help noticing just as much as he sees the hopeless gap between the American and the African negro. Racial infection is a most serious mental and moral problem where the

primitive outnumbers the white man. America has this problem only in a relative degree, because the whites far outnumber the coloured. Apparently he can assimilate the primitive influence with little risk to himself.

In the following quote by Jung, of importance is the lack of *seeing* the African American as an *American*:

> Just as the coloured man lives in your cities and even within your houses, so also he lives under your skin, subconsciously. Naturally it works both ways. Just as every Jew has a Christ complex, so every Negro has a white complex and every American a Negro complex. (*CW* vol. 10, para 963)

The above quote by Jung also holds what might be a truth observed by him in pointing out the *racial complexes* which seem evident in both races. Jungian psychology has been remiss in exploring the important relevance of these racial complexes, even though their existence was apparent to Jung decades ago. What are the nuances of racial complexes?

It is interesting to note that every other complex can be explored and amplified by American Jungians with the exception of the *racial complex* first mentioned by Jung. Why this reluctance to delve into this particular complex? My own analytical training experience is that it was completely avoided within the training of my becoming a Jungian analyst.

This might seem as if we have taken a path off of our journey in speaking of grievance to grief and perhaps we have because we are those who dwell in the underground of psyche. We know there is no place we cannot travel. We understand that the shadows that can dominate our wake ego states must be given some light of consciousness. This is the Jungian way. This way also requires us to shed the light in leading us towards a greater consciousness regarding that which keeps us hostage, caged, against a better understanding of how to treat and love our brethren—those of different ethnicities.

I believe we are in a constant movement, traveling between, above, below, around and within grievance and grief. When I first thought about the details of what I might write here I saw the journey as moving in one direction from grievance to grief but as I began to consider this journey, I saw that it was a back and forth. It was multi-directional. It contains all of the remembrances of previous travel. It contains all the archetypal grief of ancestors. The fears, the anguish and of course the blood. The spilt blood of my ancestors calls to me and speaks of grievance as well as grief.

As depth psychology travelers we have high regard for our ancestors and their stories. We love our mythologies. As American Jungians we are now more engaged than ever in searching for a light that can explore the darkened shadow of depth psychology that has included racism in its existence within the theories of American psychology. This has shown itself most blatantly in the early study and practice of Jungian dream work where every image of a person of color represented a symbol of that which was negative, undesirable and the worst of the ego.

This was the place where as Hillman stated the sociological had replaced the psychological. This was the place of psychological darkness, the underworld, where American Jungian psychology lived for many decades with no voice calling for change of light to see those of Africanist descent as more than shadow projections of a white Other.

In America since we have appropriated the color black for skin color identification, we have also appropriated all of the negative conscious and unconscious ideas related to the color black and have formed a sociological basis for projecting the negative onto those of Africanist lineage. Hillman warns us in his article "Haiti or the color black," that we must not confuse the sociological with the psychological. That our racial opinions and beliefs regarding the archetypal black of the nigredo does not belong to the Africanist individual or groups projected on and weighted down by negative sociological projections belonging to the shadow of the one who projects.

Our skin defines us and sets us apart or gathers us together like our ancestral tribes. Even those who are mixed ethnicities have been for the most part unable to avoid the haunting of racial complexes on a personal, cultural and an American collective level.

The voices of those who protested the political and social subservience of black skin to white skin first came early on from Europe. The history of the Abolitionist movement began on the European continent in 1315 when the then king of France Louis X abolished slavery. The king of Spain, Charles I, also declared an end to slavery to take place in 1542; however, this law was never passed in all the colonial states. Creating laws at such a distance from Europe to the colonies almost assured that compliance would be an issue—long before the American Revolutionary War.

The official beginning of the Abolitionist movement that was to have the most influential effect on Africanist, colonized people occurred in England in the end of the 18th century when British and later American Quakers became interested and involved in the question of morality as related to the reality of slavery. In 1772, a legal case entitled the Somersett Case, involved setting a fugitive slave free based on English Common law which stated that slavery was forbidden and therefore no one could be held in slavery. This case set the precedent for English men such as Granville Sharpe and William Wilberforce. Slavery was officially abolished in all the American northern states in 1804. International slave trade was abolished in 1807 by America and Great Britain, the British Slavery Abolition Act of 1833 abolished slavery throughout the British Empire. This is the legal background of initial European attempts to end slavery of Africanist people.

The underpinning of this movement was the Enlightenment with its focus on natural law—the idea that human beings did not require divine intervention in order to make the best decisions for themselves as regards injustices, social life and freedom. Nature could be understood without the assistance of God. Slavery had previously been justified by the proposition that God wanted and desired some to be enslaved; this idea came under question as the movement for the abolition of slavery became stronger in the years before the American Revolution. With the coming of the

American Revolution, based politically and philosophically on the tenets of Enlightenment the idea of slavery as outdated and harmful to the American political psyche was taken up by Thomas Jefferson. We are getting the irony here, right? Natural law under Enlightenment also believed in the protection of private property. Thomas Jefferson *never* gave up his slaves who birthed six of his children.

The Other: emergence from a literary shadow

Gwendolyn Brooks, Nikki Giovanni, and Sonia Sanchez were women poets of the Black Arts Movements that covered the decade, from 1960 into the early 1970s. This arts movement developed from the Black Power Movement of the 1960s when political activism gained strength under the guidance of the Black Panther power, student rights organizations and civil disobedience by ordinary citizens. The seeds thrown in the field of consciousness took root and spread from the late 1950s into a new generation coming of age in the new decade of the 1960s. As African Americans faced the continued and *continuing* challenges of a denial of voting rights, segregated public facilities and the rape of Black women and murder of Black men—all that Jim Crow could offer, rebellion began—again, in American cities. LeRoi Jones, the poet who later became known to us as Amiri Baraka, is credited with founding the Black Arts Movement said: *We want a black poem. And a Black World. Let the world be a Black Poem.* I love these words because they say everything about the energy and cultural consciousness that ripped open a literary world which was relentless in its refusal to allow for much of an admittance of black literature, certainly not black poetry. The Harlem Renaissance Movement which included poets like Langston Hughes found favor but only in a narrow stream of creative voices. It was struggling to come alive in the boldly alive days of Jim Crow. The decades between those of the Harlem Renaissance and the Black Arts Movement saw the emergence of Richard Wright, Hurston and other writers who would leave their mark on Black literature. The Black Arts Movement emerged because of those of the Harlem Renaissance who built a bridge of literary excellence upon which to cross.

The powerful force of the Black Arts Movement must be considered through the cultural lens of oppression from which it emerged. This lens had its preparation within the context of Black language being considered on a linguistic hierarchy where Black language was discredited. The struggle in opposition to segregation and disempowerment of Africanist people included the re-claiming of Africanist linguistic structures. We began to say, *I'm black and I'm proud*, with recognition of heritage of the language of our ancestors.

American Black writers began to identify and claim our linguistic roots that ran deep in the soil of West African based languages. All of the stories of how African Americans spoke gibberish and had no intelligence based on our natural speech patterns were now identified as one more way in which to discredit Africanist people. The strength of claiming Ebonics as a part of our linguistic inheritance was a major influence in the strength of claiming a Black voice for poetry. When

Baraka said, "let the world be a Black poem," his words claimed and gave power to all of us who came from the lineage of the African griot, the storyteller who told and brought our stories across the Atlantic on slave ships. We once again could see ourselves beyond the barriers of racism into an ancestral past that saw no limits even though we had arrived on America's shores in chains.

In *Injala: Sonia Sanchez and the African Poetic Tradition* (1996), author Joyce Ann Joyce says:

> Every literary period has its authors whose works defy easy, unambivalent cate-gorization. The works of Black American writers usually rest at the heart of this rule. Much of the early criticism surrounding the Black poetry that began to flourish during the sixties shows how literary criticism tends to adjudge the merit of a new, innovative work or genre by using old preconceived notions that affix the work in the quagmire of tradition.

Going a bit further in discussing an essay entitled "The New Poetry of Black Hate," Joyce states that this essay "exemplifies the misconceptions and mis-understandings that embody the Black poetry of the 1960s. Arthur Davis writer of the essay says in speaking of Black poetry: *"The newness, except for the hate motivation, is about as meaningful as the change from a 'konked' head to a bush."* Black poetry was ridiculed for its language and its relationship with the cultural and political transformation that was occurring and was dismissed.

However, encouraged by the popularity of the published writing of Gwendolyn Brooks, the first African American woman to win a Pulitzer Prize in 1950, black women writers began to have their writings receive more of a broader audience. It was through the distribution of these writings that black women would begin to gain popularity and respect in the art field. This has still not occurred within the field of visual arts. There remain a few exceptions—Kara Walker has achieved a wide-spread following. No African American visual artists has achieved the level of success as has occurred with black writers. This is, however, underscored by the fact that it took another 32 years for Alice Walker to win the Pulitzer for the *Color Purple* in 1982. Toni Morrison won the Pulitzer for her fiction book *Beloved* in 1988. The Black Arts Movement and the voice of poetry opened a literary door to make possible the emer-gence of the works of Alice Walker—herself a poet, and Toni Morrison. Both of these women established their own writing careers by writing about the Africanist experience of survival in American. Their writing is oppositional and shows the emergence of ideas and characters that speak to the need for opposition to a society structure that has embedded racism in all of its forms. In tracing the literary lineage from poet Brooks:

> This is a poem of grief—the personal grief of a mother who a woman who has lost her children through personal decisions.

Our grief as Africanist women certainly includes our loss of children. We have lost our children because we could not control their destinies due to slavery and their being the property of the slave owner. We have lost our children because we could not protect them against the ravages of Jim Crow and lynching. We have lost our children because we could not face bringing them into the world. Gwendolyn Brooks poem speaks to this in her poem, "The Mother."

Nikki Giovanni was born in 1943. This poem "Mother's Habits" is taken from her book *The Women and the Men*. This is another poem of grief and speaks to the sadness of what we inherit. In my own writing about African American women—*Archetypal Grief: Slavery's Legacy of Intergenerational Child Loss* (2018)—I address the emotional pain of intergenerational mother's loss. This I believe is an aspect of archetypal grief—the suffering we experience as part of the cultural trauma of slavery's effect on our group. I think this type of suffering is passed on from mother to daughter to mother to daughter. An endless transference of emotional pain—intergenerational mother loss and child loss.

As a cultural group, we are having more and more conversations about what our mothers could not give us. Nikki Giovanni's poem takes a difficult and hard look at what it feels like to think that one will acquire the habit of the mother. A habit that does not speak to love but one of the lack of care and caring.

As painful as it might be this is the poet's voice that I hear speaking of both grievance and grief. I think about the black women who could only really have time devoted to caring for white children. These nannies and Jemima women were forced to give their very best to white children. In the historical pictures we see them holding white children. I have rarely seen an image of a black woman holding her black child during slavery except on the auction block.

In her discussion of Sonia Sanchez, author Joyce Ann Joyce says: "Although Sanchez cites Alexander Pushkin and Federico Garcia Lorca as influences on her early poetry ... the influence of the African tradition emerges as the most sustained." Sonia Sanchez has been writing poems since the early days of the Black Arts Movement. In describing the purpose of her work she says that "... poetry is a subconscious conversation, it is as much the work of those who understand it and those who make it." Sanchez continues her work as a poet and teacher even today. She has received the Robert Frost Medal as well as numerous other awards that speak to her power as both a political influence and a creative one. The longevity of her voice to influence generations of poets has spanned decades. In 1985 Sanchez received the American book Award for her book *Homegirls and Handgrenades*.

Nikki Giovanni, a third popular woman poet of the Black Arts Movement was born in 1943 in Knoxville Tennessee. In the text *Black Sister: Poetry by black American Women, 1746–1980*, author Erlene Stetson (1981) says: Black women poets have addressed two questions: "How do we assert and maintain our identities in a world that prefers to believe we do not exist? How do we balance and contain our rage so that we can express both our warmth and love and our anger and pain?" I think that these issues faced by these poets are the questions faced by many if not all black women and men. Our lives are defined by who we are, and by who others think us to be. The authentic face behind the persona masks we wear can be revealed in the creative work that we bring into the world. Poets like Nikki Giovanni as the other women poets of her time who gained success because of their writing, revealed not only the cultural face of African Americans but also the personal identities that could perhaps best be revealed in their poetry.

Nikki Giovanni's poem "Mother's Habit's" touches that place in me where I have felt the loss of my own mother. Once again it is a poem that speaks to grief. In writing out of grief and anticipating the loss of mother, I recall the stories of my mother as a woman who bore her suffering in a silent manner that allowed not much room for empathy. Nikki Giovanni calls it caring.

African Americans have a literary history that goes before the artist movements of Black writers of the 20th century. I want to share with you a voice from our Africanist past. It is a story of our early beginnings. Four hundred years is a very long time. There are many voices that go unrecognized because they could not all fit into the history books. There were over 12 million who came across the Atlantic, of these it is estimated that 10 million survived to become slaves in the Americas and the Caribbean islands. Each one had a story. Their voices are a part of the struggle that we live today. This is the voice of one who was born into slavery, a young girl named Mary Prince, taken from the book *Six Women's Slave Narratives*.

I will share with you from when she discovers she is to be sold away at age 11 from her parents and the white family she has lived with almost since birth:

> The black morning at length came. I was soon surrounded by strange men, who examined and handled me in the same manner that a butcher would a calf or a lamb he was about to purchase, and who talked—as if I could not more understand than the dumb beasts …

The emerging self and the struggle of the ego

What about my Individuation as a poet, a writer, as a creator? How do I fit my ego self-ambitions into the necessity of being with a cultural group that has experienced grievance and profound grief? What about my cultural collective? We have suffered, and once again begin once to feel the grievance. We seem to feel it over and over again because racism always seems to be with us. If we believe Jung, complexes will always be there, this must include our racial complexes. What about our American cultural complex? We face each other in opposition in our most basic tribal way—especially today. I face myself in opposition. I want to write poems that speak not only to the telling of the stories of horror but also the grief of letting go.

> Perhaps I am still too close to the grievance. Perhaps not enough time has passed since my first ancestors stood on the auction blocks, worked the plantation fields of South Carolina. Perhaps, I will not complete this journey from grievance to grief in this lifetime.

Grievance to grief: from loss to art

How do we write not out of grievance but from and toward grief? How do we transform our losses into art even as we sometimes wrestle with healing ourselves?

In my own work as a writer I have spent time researching the history of slavery and the brutal effects of the Southern plantation slavery system. There were days, months when I had to turn away from my work, my writing because it was too painful to face the images of ancestors—my own and those of my African diaspora. There were days that I cried and couldn't write. Is it true that "The only alternative to torture is art"? as an audience once asked at a gathering. I believe this is an aspect of emergence into a field of transformation where loss is felt, painfully felt, and art emerges. If we are to believe Jung, then emergence can also be transformation in service of individuation.

Did I grow emotionally from my writing experiences of looking deep into the history and horror of slavery? I don't know. I did write, once the acute pain of my reading of slavery stopped, a book on archetypal grief—the intergenerational emotional suffering of mothering slaves. I would like to believe that this book has changed me. That it changed my consciousness in some valued way that I perhaps cannot yet understand. bell hooks in her own autobiography, Remembered Rapture: The writer at work, says:

> To engage a politics of transformation we surrender the need to occupy a space of hedonistic intellectual "cool" that covertly embraces old notions of objectivity and neutrality. Certainly I and my work are often seen as not cool enough precisely because there is always an insistence on framing ideas politically and calling for active resistance.

This work of resistance makes African American writing alive. It resonates with the necessary identity and the call and response to an inner self that requires recognition of much that has gone before. I'm not certain—still, of how to walk all the paths of grievance and grief. I want to be able to say that the movement is linear. My ego wants this and yet I know that from inside I also feel the energy of needing to push against some things that are not yet right. And there is a right.

A right way to treat others, a right way to respect the past and a right way to envision a future. This could feel like a space that lacks humility but I have learned over the years that it is true—if I don't take a stand I will fall for anything. I have fallen many times. Now I try to take a stand even when I fail. I wrote my first book because it called to me. It demanded to be written because it was the right thing to do.

I wanted to write about the Feminine and the Jungian Animus. When I wrote my thesis manuscript finalizing my Jung Institute training to be an analyst I wrote about Hina, a Hawaiian goddess who was a battered Feminine. I joined the amplification of this myth with a case study of a patient who was a battered woman. My doctoral dissertation was completed on a study of three African American Women dreamers. An important part of both of these works was my sense of putting something right—letting something new emerge that included the feel of resistance.

I believe that my being called as a writer is as equally important as being called to become a Jungian analyst. It still seems odd to me and probably always will because it was not ego alone making the decision to write about the topics I have chosen and that more importantly have chosen me.

bell hooks says:

> Dissenting and critical voices are easily co-opted by the longing to be both heard and admired, our words longed for and affirmed. Subculture stardom can be as seductive a distraction as speaking in the interests of mainstream cultural politics of domination. Critical writing that remains on the edge, able to shift paradigms, to move in new directions, subverts this tendency. It demands of critics fundamental intellectual allegiance to radical openness, to free thinking. (p. 44)

I would say for myself this is resistance—it is shadow work ... Someone at dinner last night said to me that my writing is heavy. I agreed with her. But I want to write sweet romances. I have no idea when that's going to happen.

How do we write not out of grievance but from and toward grief? How do we transform our losses into art even as we sometimes wrestle with healing ourselves?

I think that my writing is always about wrestling with healing myself. It takes me to dark places and memories that can make me cry. I say this not to get empathy but only because it is a truth—my truth. When I chose to write about Hina a battered Feminine goddess, it was because growing up I knew women who in their silence suffered battering. This part of my life emerged within the context of a Hawaiian myth. It holds my grievance as well as my grief. The writing of that manuscript was an act of resistance as well as healing. I think the personal experience of writing, creating, the things that choose us, is always a part of our necessary healing. Maya Angelou said it so beautifully when she said, "and still I rise."

I believe that Laura McCollough's above quote from her book on poetry and racism goes directly to the heart of the questions and thoughts we have regarding the topic. I think Maya Angelou's poem addresses how we must be in our resistance to children being put in cages, how we must resist a return to conservative laws that want to bring us back to days when women had no political control over their own bodies and when black people had no right to vote. We bear suffering in order to transform consciousness. This is our work as 21st-century creators, thinkers and those who can tolerate the dark in order to emerge with that which can be transformative, not just for ourselves but also for our collective.

11

AMERICAN CINEMA: *GET OUT*

The image has always been of particular importance within the theoretical foundation of depth psychology. Murray Stein in his chapter "The Populated Interior" from *Jung's Map of the Soul* (2010) quotes Jung who giving his definition of the feeling tone-toned complex: "It is the image of a certain psychic situation which is strongly accentuated emotionally and is moreover, incompatible with the habitual attitude of consciousness" (p. 48). In expanding on Jung's definition, Stein says, "Images defines the essence of psyche … The complex is an inner object, and at its core it is an image" (p. 48).

In extending and developing the imaginal space I have engaged with a film and attempt to see how an unconscious process, images, and creativity come together as a reflection black and white cultural racial complexes.

The film is *Get Out* by director Jordan Peele produced in 2017. The main characters in the film include Chris, a black young man, his white girl Rose and the young man's best friend Rod.

As the film opens we find a lone man on the street, headed to a party in an unknown to him suburban location. Talking to himself, this black man who is later identified in the film as Dre says he feels like "a sore thumb" out in the night in the suburbs. He lets the audience know that he is out of place. It is also the night—a place of the unconscious—he is lost in the dark trying to find the correct location of the place he is to be visiting. He says: "Don't do nothing stupid. You know how they like to treat motherfucker's out here." Dre has a natural cultural paranoia that he will be mistreated by a white Other. He is uncomfortable in the neighborhood—it's not his own and he has anxiety about his safety. So much so that he decides to turn around and not pursue looking for the house.

In the darkness a car pulls up behind him and follows. The music coming from the car is a song that appears to be from the 1930s or 1940s. The significance of the music is that later in the film we can see a connection between the car music and the time period of the 1930s.

Suddenly Dre is hit on the head from behind and put into the trunk of the car. This music is set against the visuals of Dre walking and being captured. As the music from the approaching car has gotten louder it is at this moment that he decides to leave and not continue to look for the house. In this first opening scene we have a black man who is captured and stolen. This establishes the narrative for the film.

In the next scene we see tall trees as if the viewer is driving along watching them pass. The music accompanying the woodsy trees scene is an African rhythm and is changed from the opening musical score that was a vocalization from the 1930s.

The next scene is of Chris the main character at home shaving, stark white shaving cream against his black skin. His girlfriend Rose is shown at the bakery. We may or may not know that they are connected in some way until she appears at his front door. As he packs, he asks her if her parents who they are planning to visit, knows that he is black. She tells him that they do not know he is black. She says that they are not racist or she wouldn't be bringing him home to meet them. This is the first time that Rose tells Chris a lie.

Rod calls Chris while Rose drives. He warns him that he should not be going into the country with a white girl friend to her family's house. He refers to his own paranoia. I would call this a *cultural paranoia*. His is the voice that indicates the possible peril of trusting his white girl friend (too) much. Once again the image is of the woods. Chris and Rose are driving to the parents. Suddenly, the car hits an object and stops. It is a deer from which they can hear a death cry from a distance. Rose stands in the road as Chris follows the sound of the deer. He tears up. Rose never leaves the side of the car.

In the next scene the policeman is there, asks to see Chris's identification. Rose defends Chris saying that he doesn't have to show his identification. Chris gives it over to the policeman without any protest. Back in the car Rose says, "I'm not gonna let anyone fuck with my man." This is paradoxical we will later see as the story develops.

Upon arrival to the house, the parents greet Rose and Chris with friendly chatter, showing Chris family pictures. One significant image is noted by Rose's father. He shows a picture of his own father Roman Armitage who lost the running race in 1934 to Jesse Owens at the Berlin Olympics.

Chris is unable to sleep after dinner and goes out to have a smoke. It has already been discussed at dinner where the husband has recommended that Chris undergo hypnosis to get rid of this habit. His wife has provided successful treatment for him.

On his way back in from outside Chris encounters Rose's mother who invites him into her office. She begins to ask him pointed questions regarding the day of his mother's death. Chris begins to cry. A part of the hypnosis is the tap with a spoon to the teacup. Chris reports that he feels paralyzed as the day his mother was hit by a car on her way home from work.

Unknowingly, he sat in front of the television watching while she died outside in the cold. With what Mrs. Armitage calls "heightened suggestibility," Chris finds himself falling out of the chair into a black space which looks like nighttime outer space with stars. In the distance he can see Mrs. Armintage as if framed by a television screen. Chris tries to catch a hold of something as he falls. He only grasps empty space. Later, he in wakes up in bed.

The next day as they are served lunch by a black woman servant Georgina. The parents says how her mother loved the kitchen so much and so they keep the servant as "a piece of her in here," the kitchen. This is another instance of paradoxical truth and lie in the film as told by a character.

Later when Chris speaks to Rose he tells her that he has met another servant, Walter, and he appears jealous of him in their discussion of Rose. She begins to tease him and their scene eventually leads to a sexual one.

Guests begin to arrive for the weekend. Rose explains to Chris that she didn't know they were coming and doesn't really want them to be there.

Later we discover that this too is a lie.

As guests stand around and begin to speak with Chris he finds their language to him unusually racial. He is asked about his golf grip, Tiger Woods—"let's see your form." Someone remarks on his black sin which is now "in fashion" because the "pendulum swung back."

Chris then meets another guest, Jim Hudson a blind photography gallery owner. Hudson knows Chris's work as a photographer and says, "I'm an admirer of your eye." Upon leaving Hudson, Chris returns upstairs to his bedroom to once again find his phone unplug. Chris then calls his friend Rod who says white hypnosis would have him barking like a dog or flying in the air, he says they make sex slaves out of black people. He says he doesn't want them getting in his head like Jeffrey Dolmar.

The phone connection dies and Georgina enters the room apologizing to Chris for leaving his phone unplugged. He says he gets nervous with too many white people as they will rat you out. Georgina begins to silently cry while repeated saying the word "no." You can see an inner struggle as she tries to regain what appears to be control between the tears and obvious suffering and the word she keeps repeating. Finally she regains composure and says, "They trust us like family." Chris determines as she walks away that she is "crazy."

Returning back downstairs, in his obvious discomfort of references to his body with the other guests, Chris sees a black male guest who is introduced as Logan. The "bump" Chris handshake offers Logan is returned as a regular handshake. Christ is surprised by the lack of "brotherly" communication. A few minutes later Chris takes a flash photo of Logan who suddenly runs to him with a nosebleed and screams at Chris to "get out." The Armintage son overcomes Logan and in the next scene the latter is apologizing for his behavior.

Rose decides to take Chris on a walk to the lake where Chris says he wants to leave her family house and that he loves Rose. He tells her about the distress of having left his mother by the side of the road—nobody was looking for her. He says that he will not abandon Rose to her family and will not leave without her. She says that she will go with him.

At the house, a silent "bingo game" is being played. The guests seated hold up their bingo cards as the host uses fingers to count. Finally he arrives at a count of 20 and the bingo game ends.

Upon their return to the house the guests are all leaving. Chris has sent Rod the picture he took of Logan who now tells Chris he recognizes him the black man who had disappeared months before as Dre. The phone battery dies, and the call ends. Chris is suddenly very agitated and tells Rose they must leave immediately. She goes downstairs and upstairs Chris finds in an open closet a box with many pictures of other black men and even a picture of Georgina with Rose.

As they attempt to leave with Rose saying she is unable to find the car keys, the three other members begin to crowd Chris. He fights the brother when the mother taps the teacup and he falls back to the floor in a hypnotic trance.

Chris awakes to find himself tied to a chair in the basement of the house. In front of him is a television with a stuffed deer head above the television. He tries to free himself but cannot. When he wakes again he sees a video of Roman Armitage, the father who had run against Jesse Owens explaining his technique and the "Coagula." He advises Chris not to fight it and says that one day he might enjoy being a part of the family.

Rod goes to the police station where he tries to explain that Chris has been kidnapped, brainwashed. The officers laugh at him and dismiss his story. One of the officers says, "Oh white girls, they get you every time."

Chris wakes up a second time to find that Hudson, the gallery owner is on the screen. He explains to Chris that the process he is undergoing is in three stages: hypnosis, mental preparation and finally the brain transference surgery. Chris will become a "passenger" in the "sunken place" and Hudson will retain control in terms of motor control. Chris asks, "Why us?"

"Why black people?" Hudson responds with his own question: "Who knows ... Maybe you are stronger?" Then he makes it more personal by saying that he wants Chris's eyes, the things that he sees through.

Chris eventually escapes from the basement by pulling cotton from the arms of the chair and putting it in his ears to block the sound of the teacup. He escapes to the car after killing the father, son and mother. Rose pursues him but Chris hits Georgina as he drives away. He has to decide whether to pick her up or leave her. He decides to bring her back to the car. When she awakens she screams at him that he has ruined her home. Chris crashes the car and Rose with a shotgun appears to shoot Chris. Walter appears, takes the gun and says he will kill Chris who then uses his flash camera. Walter turns on Rose, shoots her then shoots himself. A car with flashing lights appear and Rose begins to yell for help but it is not the police but Rod. Chris gets in the car. Rod: "I told you not to go in that house."

The film has an alternative ending. In the second ending it is the police who come and Chris is arrested. In the final scene Chris is seen in prison walking back to his cell after a visit by Rod.

The alternative

In beginning at the end of the film, I can understand why the film would have two possible endings. I think of this not only within the context of how the daily life can go—in fact few options are possible. Within the context of the film and the black character's life there are two options—freedom or imprisonment. This appears to be the choice from the very beginning of the film. I see this option as the first black character, Dre enters the frame—he is lost and feeling the pressure of being out of his depths in a neighborhood that is clearly white. He can leave it and have his freedom by returning to a different neighborhood or he can remain. By the time he makes his decision to leave it is too late. Desire for that which is different and a willingness to pursue it come into conflict. Dre decides in favor of his cultural self that I imagine is safe from the white suburban area in which he has found himself.

Dre and Chris, both black men who explore the territory of whiteness, find themselves at odds with this environment. Rod is the black man who has the clear perspective, itself different from the other two men, on his place in the society. His warnings based on cultural paranoia are dismissed. The cultural racial complex of all three men are evidenced by their behaviors but not without consequences. In all of their ways however, it is Rod who fares the best—even with his shaming in the police station as they laugh at his "preposterous" idea that his black friend has been taken as a sex slave by Rose and her family. In this contemporary film, the shadow of slavery's theme is over not just this idea of Chris being stolen into (sex) slavery but also the woodsy scene reminiscent of a southern landscape as well as the bingo auction.

Get Out is a visual journey through a lens of current slavery, human frailty and our cultural racial complexes. Chris appears naive in his refusal to not trust his friend Rod. In the relationship, he is Chris's shadow—the alter ego that refuses to listen to a deeper inner voice. The voice of Self pushes to a deeper learning experience—no matter how painful. Chris's path must continue to unfold and he must learn to endure whatever is on the path to greet him. We find that his childhood is a major aspect of what is still held in shadow for him. His subtle seduction by Mrs. Armintage and her teacup is the archetypal mother possession that allows this because of the trauma of the death of his mother. The mother complex is triggered with one of guilt in Chris believing that he has failed to save his mother's life or that she could have at least been comforted in her dying through his presence on the roadside. As he falls, the image is one of his body in space that reminds me of the heaven's constellation. He becomes constellated under the hypnosis and loses control over himself and his ability to return to consciousness from this state. Psychologically, the mother complex has taken control of him and his struggle is useless. Each time Chris does return from this "constellated" state it is because he is brought back by Mrs. Armintage, he is never able to return to consciousness on his own until through ego functioning he discovers that taking cotton from the arm of the chair and putting it in his ears will free him from hearing the sound of teaspoon to china, the auditory sound for his trance. The symbol of cotton as a way to his freedom signifies the beginning of a reversal in the main character's consciousness. He is able to use that which historically has been a symbol of black enslavement to free himself from the television, the deer and the basement. He is also able to kill the white father who holds him prisoner.

In his newly found strength—out of naivety, he can overcome the surgeon father as well as his son. As Chris moves to the upper area of the house he encounters Mrs. Armintage who he has to fight with in order to break her cup and her spell over him.

Just before they race to get the cup Chris recognizes that he cannot trust her and we can see hesitation on his face—the conflict over wanting to trust the mother.

Almost through instinct of survival he runs to the cup. In the physical struggle that develops he no longer hesitates and stabs her. This is one expression of victory of the Self in defense against a feminine archetypal energy that wishes to destroy. The second instance is when he attempts to drive away from the house and Georgina awakens after Chris stops to bring her body into the car. In their struggle he does not hesitate to hit her in his own defense. The evolution of his consciousness is terms of the feminine and a mother complex is shown in the scene where Rose has been shot. Chris kneels next to her putting his hands on her and begins to choke her. She smiles as if welcoming Chris—as if casting judgment onto him, as if she suspected he would have done nothing less. Chris stops choking her. Chris's relationship of complexes related to his mother is transforming. He has "rescued" his mother (childhood) Georgina from the road, rescued himself from the one that would have killed him (Mrs. Armintage), and not abandon himself (Soul) by choking Rose to death.

A theme of alternatives and our willingness to engage with our human lives through the film as does the overtones of slavery. There are alternatives offered by the choices that the characters must make. We see this first in Dre who must decide to continue walking into the threatening darkness of the white suburb or return to his known world. Chris is warned by Rod to get out before he fully enters into the world of the Armintages.

He has had a choice whether to follow his friend's advice or to go visit Rose's family. His identity is in question as he chooses to be the black boyfriend who goes deeper into the relationship with Rose. He could have remained within his own cultural group but chose otherwise. The film shows Chris as one character struggling with being awake or asleep—unconscious. Georgina appears to struggle especially in the scene with Chris when she repeatedly says "no" to him finally concluding that we (she and the Armintages) are like family. The struggle we see in this character is showing Chris's own struggle—mother complex, identity, safety.

Dre as Logan, after being photographed has a nose bleed—ego discrimination, clarity when he screams for Chris to get out. There is a choice and now Dre seeing this choice wants to warn Chris. Parallel alternatives are shown by the Sunken World versus the non-hypnotic state of every day existence that only Rod occupies. Chris appears to be caught between these two worlds as is shown by his seduction by Mrs. Armintage and final return to clarity as he physically begins to fight his way out of her house.

The film opens with images of Chris's work as a photographer. He chooses to shoot culturally related images reflecting his own spirit self. A third theme of the film seems to be vision. How is it operative within the characters, the gaze of the viewer and how we can see plot? Hudson, the blind gallery owner wants Chris's eyes.

When he appears on the television screen in the basement he details for Chris the process of what has been happening—the steps. It is the character that wants to see very badly that he has paid 20 million dollars for Chris's body that defines the process that will lead to his obtaining Chris's eyes. The importance in the film is put on the ability to see which we as audience can observe is limited in Chris. Even though he apparently has talent and is known for his photography—described as graphic and brutal—Chris himself lacks vision in terms of a psychologically healthy survival. The deer dies in the woods after being hit by their car. His mother dies and he leaves the safety of a culturally related mothering figure and turns to a white one. This is a choice and it comes with deadly risks. The challenge for the main character is to begin to see with different eyes. His vision from the Sunken World is anxiety producing—he is in a free-fall. All that he has previously seen has gone away from him and he has nothing to hold onto in this falling state.

The police appear in three scenes of the film. First at the roadside killing of the deer, then at the police station with Rod and last in the film's alternative ending scene. The tension that Chris seems to feel when the white policeman approaches the car runs opposite to the boldness of Rose's words to the policeman. As a white woman she doesn't have to fear the police. Rod's decision to seek police help with black officers shows his cultural trust this is betrayed. The credibility of all police officers is shadowed. One officer presents a routinely racist demand for Chris's identification, even though he was not driving the car. The black officers refuse to take a black need and call for help with any seriousness. Both of these scenes depict aspects of behaviors activated by a racial complex—black and white.

The themes of *Get Out* directly address racial cultural complexes that result from slavery and its aftermath. This film explores not only the personal unconscious material of the mother but also the associative aspects of life. Ambiguity regarding a mother who abandons through death is equally as powerful to explore as the surviving son who finds no place within for sufficient self-nurturance. The partner he does choose, Rose is actually a reflection of an inner self-hatred that seeks to kill him. He must fight for his survival.

One reality of Chris as shown in the film is actually the lived reality of hundreds of thousands of black incarcerated men. One ending to the film where Rod says to Chris I told you so is offered against the scene where Chris has to look Rod in the eyes in the prison visit and *see* his mistake. The constellation, alternative disruption and view from a cultural perspective is that the lens is always colored by a racial complex. This complex lives within us and shows itself through our behaviors. The film shows this through all of the characters. We can be seduced, hypnotized by the "richness" of white. It can blind us to its shadow. Dre, in the darkness found himself. It was also him out of all three of the "transferred" characters that we saw who was able to "breakthrough" in public and have some consciousness before once again being subdued into his hypnotic state.

Chris's alternative choices are those that the ego faces in daily life as a black man. There is no escape from the confrontation with white privilege that sets limits—a policeman, a wealthy owner who can buy you, a seductive search for romance in a lover when projected out becomes life threatening.

Racial complexes survive unconsciously and live through us whether in imagination on film or within our individual and cultural psyches. There does not seem to be a way to ever truly get out of our complexes.

12

THE PARADOX OF RACE AND RACISM

The paradox of race and racism

The first thing we must always remember is that human beings are one race. We are made up of true and also falsely constructed ethnic differences that have prolonged our suffering as members of the human race. That we are one race is not paradoxical thinking and rather straight forward. I think that we hear so often about different "races" of people that we think right away about our separations—how we are not connected. When deciding on a title for *The Racial Complex*, I remembered a conversation from a few years ago with a friend. He spoke of how in some parts of the world it is natural to think of people being of different "races." This surprised me because even in America with all of our ethnic differences, I don't see many proposing that we are different races—even when we say that someone is of "another race." Perhaps, this is because of our renewed sensitivity regarding a variety of cultures and ethnic groups. The selection of my book title then has its own paradoxical signifier of ambiguity, similar to the chapter's theme.

In my training to become a Jungian analyst, Jung's thinking was frequently called paradoxical by my instructors. Sometimes even contradictory. None of the analyst-instructors were bothered in any way by this; in fact it seem to put them in a "good mood," more of a relaxed conversational way to opening a discussion. They indicated that it was important that we learn and understand about paradoxical thinking as it was a main feature of Jung's work and what would eventually be a part of our clinical work with patients. This proved to be correct in how the subtlety of the paradoxical flowed very easily after a time into supporting patients to understand their lives and all of the inherent ambiguities. Oftentimes the paradoxes of the life appeared as disloyalty to patient. The work was in helping them develop different eyes—perhaps more intuitive or sensing, for seeing their lives. This way they could most times feel into compassion for themselves as well as those they felt had harmed them by way of a betrayal. Jung says that we must experience the "widening of consciousness beyond the narrow confines of a tyrannical intellect." (*CW* vol. 13, para 7) His belief was that every part of the human life must be experienced, including consciousness, in a fullness that could was not dictated by chiefly intellectual functioning. There needed to be an opportunity for the intuitive and instinctive selves to also take leadership as we engaged with our environment and other human beings. Jung also believed that an understanding of paradox was key to being in connection with our spiritual and religious selves. There are religious mysteries that we are asked to take on faith. This faith generally requires an acceptance of that which appears paradoxical. The blending of paradox and faith move together in a pattern of increased tolerance for ambiguity and patience with oneself.

Jung says that paradox holds the tension of the Opposites. We grow into understanding how this theory of opposites within a frame of paradox supports creating tension on a conscious level. Opposites as happening within the individual and deals with the psychological pressure of the conflicts we inherit as humans. These conflicts can arise in as simple a way as choosing between two different items for breakfast or the painful throes of making decisions regarding the divorce of a ten-year marriage. The level of intensity varies but the quality of energy of knowing the oppositional remains the same.

We are used to holding the tension of opposites within us on a psychological level. When we cannot do this we seek guidance. When this becomes of little or no use, depending on the intensity of the inner pressure, we can explode, harming ourselves, or others. I would say that this is probably after the constellation of complexes.

> A complex results from the blend of archetypal core and human experience and we feel according to our complexes. Sometimes we experience the content of the complex only in projection. Regarded dynamically, the complex may be in conflict with what we consider reality to be or with what we see as ideal—so that psychic activity is interfered with ... Structurally, the complex can be studied in relation to the ego. There may be conflict ('two truths') or the ego may repress the complex or, conversely, be overwhelmed by it. The complex can become completely dissociated from the personality, as in psychotic breakdown. (Andrew Samuels, *Jung and the Post-Jungians*, p. 48)

The conflict that we experience inwardly can then be known to erupt into our outer world. The suffering from both inner and outer is measured by many different factors. Much has to do with the darkness of shadow regarding the material that is emerging and perhaps the extent of inner repression of the material. In the way of paradox, the ego's attempt to keep psychological self-knowing hidden can be for long periods of time—into adulthood. However, psyche's attempt at balance of consciousness almost demands that which is in shadow be revealed if the intensity of the oppositional energy is too strong. The struggle to keep things hidden, in the dark, in shadow becomes too much for the ego and enters conscious awareness as an autonomous complex. The tension of the opposites can create a deeper understanding of the personal struggle that has just been played out for full ego viewing.

When this happens there can be an experience of what has defined as the transcendent function. The inner conflict has resolved itself in a healing actually because of increased psychic tension. This is paradoxical and shows itself within the clinical work. The expectation would that this type of conflict could go unresolved forever. However, the psychological work being completed with attention and focus by the therapist and client helps to increase the level of intensity for psychological issues. Within this context the opposite (whatever seeks avoidance) is revealed and encountered through the analysis. Through revelation rather than avoidance, some emotional peace can be felt by the patient. The fear of elevated and increasing psychic tension, due to the clinical work, is most times palpable in the phenomenological field, the transference and even in the patient and analyst dreams. The fear itself must be discovered at its deepest level in order that it will be less of a trigger for causing neurosis and or the setting off of complex constellations. To the ego that may have spent many years protecting itself and its personal unconscious material, the attempts of the analytical work for exposing the neurosis appears in conflict. This is partially why the patient's defenses against the analytical work that can be seen in the transference and dreams, suddenly becomes much greater. It is almost as if the patient is fighting against the psychological relief they came to therapy to achieve.

When we consider the tension between cultural groups we encounter the Opposites on a larger scale especially if we are addressing racism or racial relations. In speaking of neuroscience and our natural tendency to mirror another, I believe that this tendency can be overridden when very intense emotions are engaged.

This would be especially true as the individuals engaged in the emotional encounter are increased. The number of individuals confronting one group brings up the instinctive tribal impulse to protect one's own people—cultural group.

The type of racism that has been our American collective inheritance continues to have an oppositional quality. The cultural racial complexes that drive this opposition operate from a paradoxical frame of reference. We are ethnically different and yet humanly the same in more ways than we most times can see. Racism, consciously taught by years of falsehoods and fed by unconscious fears and complexes makes us fail to see the paradox within our relationships. There are rules to paradoxical thinking as related to racial relations as well as cultural racial complexes. Jung in his initial writing only provided us with the barest minimum of the racial complex. He wrote in a way that expressed negative opinions regarding Africanist people but only within the context of this complex to say that they would like to be white. As Michael Vannoy Adams has noted in his chapter titled "The Color Complex," from *The Multicultural Imagination: Race, Color and the Unconscious*, Jung was not the first to write about African Americans as regards what psychiatrist John Lind called the *color complex*. In referring to Lind, author of the article "The Color Complex in the Negro" in the initial issue of the *Psychoanalytic Review* (1914), Adams says the following:

In an effort to describe the psyche of African-Americans, Lind thus combines Freudian fulfillment of wishes, Jungian disturbances of reaction in relation to unconscious complexes, and Adlerian compensation of inferiority. For

African-Americans, "reality" is a social construction by white Americans. As Lind says, African-Americans occupy a socially subordinate position that white Americans have constructed on the basis of a "racial" distinction, the difference in skin color. The inferiority complex of African-Americans is, in this sense, a reflection of inferior status. The psychical reality of African-Americans is thus a function of social reality. African-Americans might simply accept this social reality, this inferior status, but many do not. Instead, they reject it. They fail to adapt, as it were, and construct an alternative, psychical reality (in some cases, a delusional, psychotic reality) in which, as if in a dream, they fulfill a wish to be white—that is, to be equal to whites (or superior to blacks). What is, in Freudian terms, a wish-fulfillment is, in Adlerian terms, an inferiority compensation. (Adams, 1996, pp. 122–123)

The earliest writings within the American psychoanalytical movement were from whites psychiatrists who did their studies with mentally ill hospitalized patients, who fantasized about being white and thus what he termed a "color complex" psychosis.

This racial complex description by Lind was given greater detail than in Jung's mere mention of a negro and a white complex. However, the main idea was there: African Americans wanted to be white. The addition to this theory for Jung was that whites by having been "touched" by blacks now had the latter "subconsciously" under their white skin. According to Lind any resemblance between African Americans and whites is due to a "talent for mimicry, recalling to us in some measure our jungle cousins" (p. 125).

The paradox of Opposites comes into play with the theory of blacks wanting to be white. The proposal that blacks would exchange their skin color requires thinking that pushes blacks into the opposite of who they really were in their true lives. The "clinical" studies completed by Lind on African American hospitalized patients all claiming either to be white or desirous of being white, does not hold any validity or reality since Lind himself appears to be caught in a "superiority" complex indicative of a white cultural complex that shows hatred of a black Other. This shows the paradoxical thinking of a cultural white racial complex in activation that does not see into its own unconscious shadow material.

This was not unusual for the beginning of American psychoanalysis as a field and its definition of African Americans. The creation of a black Other who was made inferior was paradoxical in that this Other was not actually in existence. It was a made-up illusion as a creation of a cultural white complex developing "scientific" proof as to black peoples "inferiority" for the bolstering of their own scientific superior knowledge.

The rules of the racial complex—autonomy, repression, eruption, amnesia, and associative impulses are aspects of racial paradox. The white cultural complex exhibited through the use of racism and avenues of power within the American collective, literally wish that blacks have no power—in whatever way this is possible known to our collective. In having this repressed wish—which is more oftentimes now spoken of as an aspect of white liberalism, means that black consciousness increases its demands for power. As cultural group awareness becomes greater so does the development of ego awareness and finding ways to create more success in achieving power. The behavioral moments in history for example would be the increase in voting power which elected Barack Obama to the presidency. The reaction to this display of power has consistently been the attempt to manipulate voter turnout and political rights by blacks to decrease their increase in political power at the ballet box. However, the rise in white cultural racial complex fear of loss of power paradoxically causes the rise in black consciousness.

The paranoia that accompanies black people as a cultural paranoia—maybe part of their racial complex is paradoxical in that the necessity for it is both true and false. Blacks must be paranoid because I believe this is a feature of living in a racist society.

I believe this to be truth that has not disappeared over the centuries. It is also a falsity that they can blindly accept the American Dream and all that it supposedly offers to them as American citizens. So their paranoia shows up as unnecessary based on the hopes for realizing an American Dream that is impossible to achieve due to racism.

African Americans live a paradoxical existence as American citizens. This has been from the considerations of identity since arriving as slaves. This paradoxical situation is also touched by the fact of blacks as historic economic "possessions" for the financial improvement of whites. How can African Americans be considered valuable producers of their own economic success when the collective still thinks of them as either inferior "producers" or only consumers to boost white financial success?

Whites who have their paranoia about blacks are in the same category. They are afraid of blacks due perhaps to a guilt complex, an inferiority complex that speaks to their unconscious psychic intergenerational material that still lives within their psyche. They have a right to these perhaps unrealized unconscious fears while "holding" all the power where there should be nothing to fear.

African Americans have learned to live with the paradoxical because in many ways American life is a sociologically paradoxical place in terms of race. The comfort of the black culture group is that there is a chance to rest from the wearying struggle to be "free" and still have freedom, to be financially stable without being acknowledged as one who is financially capable of stability—the list goes on and on. This is in a way being marginalized—to know one's truth and yet in each moment to be living a matching integrated falsehood. It's exhausting to the ego.

Racism on both the conscious and unconscious levels can cause activation that makes one paranoid, dissociated and distrustful of the self as well as society's institutions. This is deeply disturbing to individuals and to any cultural group that still struggles with survival.

13

HEALING CULTURAL AND RACIAL TRAUMA

We know that trauma has happened to and with the African diaspora. I state this very clearly because even in our collective today there are those who wish to deny the impact of this cultural trauma on Africanist people. I don't have any particular desire to remain focused on this aspect of Africanist life any longer than necessary. As previously stated, unfortunate for all of us, we have just only now begun to have even the briefest of conversations regarding this trauma. I do believe we have a much better opportunity to begin to consider ways of healing if we can first acknowledge our pain.

One of the tenets of Jungian psychology is that what poisons us will also heal us. The idea that the serpent—symbol of medicine, holds the remedy and this can be life-restoring is a significant one for reminding us of the necessity to embody both poison and remedy. This proposed idea keeps the focus from wandering away from the necessary suffering that occurs with the poison—the psychic physical and mental trauma.

In recognition of the racial complex as a cause of trauma—both individual and collective, because that is the nature of the complex—it is possible to view this trauma as holding the salve for our communal healing. I understand that complexes are a part of our psychic reality. They do not disappear because this is what we wish. I think that is our first entry into considering healing. Our idea regarding healing and what it looks like might have to change. There is no complete place of wholeness when all is resolved and we have ended suffering from trauma. We can find moments of peace and relief.

The cause of racial trauma continues to be activated and constellated in our lives by racist behaviors—whether on the political level or within our churches. In the news today is the announcement of the death of 290 people in Sri Lanka as retaliation from a white group who attempted mass murder in Christchurch Australia two months ago. I view this as another moment of a collective complex constellation. We cannot stop the painful trauma now being felt by the families of those who were murdered and in those of us who can feel the senseless killing being done in the name of politics.

What can we do about cultural and collective healing?

Perhaps a second way in which we can begin to approach our healing is accepting that there are some who couldn't care less about healing our trauma—cultural or collective. They also might not care about healing our ocean or our planet. We have our differences and I don't think we can afford to spend too much more time disputing with anyone, making someone an Other in defense of an individual or cultural difference. I think those who are willing must turn their gaze towards a task of healing that has intentionality. I think this is living a purposeful life that may help us with cultural healing.

The trauma of the African Holocaust belonged to us for a very long time—centuries. We will not nor cannot forget it as a part of our cultural healing. In fact it is essential for our healing. We will also never forget because we continue to live in the 21st-century reality of a racism that was bred and grown due to the African Holocaust.

Barbara Fletchman Smith in *Transcending the Legacies of Slavery: A Psychoanalytic View* says, "Transcending the legacies of slavery is a difficult matter. This is due to the circularity of the trauma left behind, but it is possible and necessary to transcend it … Transcending slavery does not mean forgetting or refusing to know" (pp. 105–106).

It is of the utmost importance to hold the collective memory of the cultural experience of the African Holocaust. The future children of those living today deserve to know their past and how they have come to live the lives they will be living. I think that letting go of the past discredits the future of generations to come. In taking the long view of Africanist history before and since arriving in America, the African diaspora who survived for centuries have continued to create and re-create their existence. The goal is always to make a better life for the descendants that are to come. One of the most powerful ways we can do this is to have a conscious awareness that holds this as a goal—not only the survival of life but also the spirit and value that Africanist people have merited by the fact of this long life.

Another reason we will not be able to forget our trauma is because it is a trauma that not only lives unconsciously but also has the power of autonomy. This type of power means that all of the racialized archetypal and associative memories that appear as behavior recede back into shadow where it is forgotten. This forgetting is only temporary as the deeper issues that might cause a transformation of the racial complex and its trauma cannot be tolerated. Not in seeing it. Not in discussion. Not in ownership. Speaking about the suffering of a holocaust gives the racial complex less of a place to hide.

After the Jewish Holocaust, there were pictures of Auschwitz and other former concentration camps, films, broad and deep discussions, memorials, and much more to support the words, *we will never forget*. There is an International Holocaust Remembrance Day on January 27th of each year. Those who wish to forget or say that the Jewish Holocaust never occurred have been given little power to negate such a culturally traumatic event.

It is only now that there is beginning to be remembrances of all the millions of Africanist people who died through the centuries due to the African Holocaust.

Though a national slave memorial has initially proposed in Congress in 2003, the bill to create such a memorial has not been approved. Perhaps, as a conciliation, the National Museum of African American History and Culture opened in Washington, D.C. in 2016. For those who see this as an unnecessary homage to the millions of Africans and African Americans who have died as a result of slavery, I would say that it is but one very small beginning towards our collective healing. The reason for such a lengthy healing has been the absence of a sincere enough honoring of those within the cultural group who suffered. The African tradition of recognizing the dead as leaving only the body behind not the spirit recognizes that all ancestors must be honored. The African Holocaust was a dishonoring of every part of African culture. The resultant time to heal and think about conscious healing will perhaps take equally as long. I think the time for healing comes because of memory and our willingness to remember. This would be not only to remember but also to allow for grieving. In the writing of my last book, I spent months prior to writing it, caught in a space of grieving for the ancestral women of whom I was writing (Brewster, 2018). We cannot escape suffering especially when it is of the magnitude such as a holocaust.

How can we obtain healing of equal magnitude?

What has been the greatest suffering—in what area of Africanist life? How do we take measurement?

I'm uncertain I can answer any of these questions and I believe we must begin to ask more of these questions in order for more collective healing to occur. Fletchman Smith (2011) says:

> Slavery's longest-lasting legacy is the dominant family structure that it shaped. There is no escaping the fact that slavery determined how the family formed in the Caribbean, and its repercussions are still with us today. The negative aspects of this dominant structure need not persist. Present-day problems with forming couples and making and maintaining families have everything to do with the historical past of the individual and society. Slavery by nature was responsible for the introduction of a deficit in maternal care, combined with the introduction of excessive fear into the mind. (p. xii)

The author, a black British woman of Caribbean descent addresses the main issue as she observes it within her duties as a psychotherapist. Her book details the suffering of her patients and allows them to work within a cultural framework that promotes healing through a recognition of the initial trauma of a racial complex and archetypal event of slavery. It appears that though these aspects of the clinical work being laid as ground work, the clinician is able to clearly see how the historical past of the patients have influenced their contemporary lives. There is no avoidance to seeing the impact on her patients. Within the clinical work, everyone is engaged in the real relationship.

In America we have had a great difficulty seeing into the suffering of Africanist people due to the holocaust. The denial has been of such epic proportions that centuries have passed with just living with the "cover-up." I think this is why bringing more shadowed issues as this denial into our consciousness applies a necessary sensibility to how we might begin to heal faster. I'm not speaking of achieving wholeness from working on the complex. I'm addressing opening up the conversations regarding our shadow material that continues to hide as it shows itself in racist behaviors in public through the activation of the racial complex. I believe that the recognition of unconscious processes such as the racial complex would move us along in a teleos way that points to healing. Isn't it better to know what you are facing? In the clinical work a significant indicator of positive change is the when the client can begin to identify her/his own pattern of avoidance and is willing to see into their own shadowed unconscious material. The recognition of acting out behaviors based on a complex shines a light on how to create less personal suffering. I suggest this as another way that we may consider healing on both an individual as well as a collective level.

Marco Iacoboni in *Mirroring People: The Science of Empathy and How We Connect with Others* (2008) says that we are actually built to be with another in an emotionally related manner. Iacoboni in writing of his theory of this relatedness says:

> My theory of how mirror neurons become the neural glue between self and other starts with the development of mirror neurons in the infant brain. Although there are no empirical data available yet, a very likely scenario is not hard to surmise. Baby smiles, the parent smiles in response. Two minutes later, baby smiles again, the parent smiles again. Thanks to the imitative behavior of the parent, the baby's brain can associate the motor plan necessary to smile and the sight of the smiling face. Therefore—presto! Mirror neurons for a smiling face are born … Indeed, according to this account, mirror neurons in the infant brain are formed by the interactions between self and other. (p. 34)

Marco Iacoboni (2008) asks the question many of us do. If we are programmed for empathy with one another then why are we not getting along better? Why do we kill one another—make the other suffer with such consistency?

The neuroscientist's response is that there are three reasons for this to happen. The first reason is that "In the phenomenon of imitative violence that the same neurological mechanisms facilitating empathy may produce under specific circumstances and contexts, a behavior that is the opposite of an empathetic behavior" (p. 288). The author states that "this is mostly a hypothesis right now, but it is a very strong one" (p. 269). He further says that even going beyond hypothesis, policy making and the economics of drug-making that goes towards neurological treatment for patients will win out over any concern for decreasing collective violence.

The second reason that Iacoboni gives for perhaps a disinterest in public policy formulations that would be helpful in using neuroscience findings and research towards decreasing violence:

> Mirror neurons are premotor neurons, and thus are cells not really concerned with our reflective behavior. Indeed, mirroring behaviors such as the chameleon

effect seem implicit, automatic, and pre-reflective. Meanwhile, society is obviously built on explicit, deliberate, reflective discourse. Implicit and explicit mental processes rarely interact; indeed, they can even dissociate. However, the neuroscientific discovery of mirror neurons has disclosed the pre-reflective of understand other people ... People say that they are moved to sadness when they watch a tearjerker film; they are moved to joy when their child hits a home run and celebrates after rounding the bases. I some literal sense they are indeed moved. There is something like physical contact when they orchestrate movements in their mind when watching someone. People seem to have the intuition that "being moved" is the basis of empathy and thus morality. (p. 270)

The author provides a third reason as to why our mirroring network fails to stop us from harming one another:

True cross-cultural encounters are actually made impossibly by the influence of massive belief systems—religious and political—that deny continuously the fundamental neurobiology that links us together. (p. 271)

This third and last reason given by Iacoboni points to that physical place in us because of religion or beliefs overrides our biological instinct for being in empathy with another. This empathy that sits with us in a clinical setting, with family we care about or helping a stranger fails to emerge when we are overcome with complex material from our unconscious.

How can we best work with neuroscience as we consider the racial complex with its emotionality, will-power and associative trauma(s)?

Killing Rage: Ending Racism (1995) was written by bell hooks in a decade of what was an "obvious" fear of black rage. One of the emotions—anger, that has produced in current times the creation of hate crime laws is based on the irrational expression of angry violence against another. In today's world, we are still conditioned to an idea of black rage even as we see more blacks harmed at the hands of whites. In the unconscious and then made conscious world of a white cultural complex being triggered, by the dismissal of those who harm black children and adults escaping prosecution, we are continuously instructed that black rage is unacceptable. White rage is acceptable.

Hooks says:

The rage of the oppressed is never the same as the rage of the privileged. One group can change their lot only by changing the system; the other hopes to be rewarded within the system. Public focus on black rage, the attempt to trivialize and dismiss it, must be subverted by public discourse about the pathology of white supremacy, the madness it creates. *We need to talk seriously about ending racism if we want to see an end to rage.* White supremacy is frightening. It promotes mental illness and various dysfunctional behaviors on the part of whites and non-whites. It is the real and present danger—not black rage. (p. 30)

My talking and writing about racism within the context of Jungian psychology and the racial complex is because I trust in processes that are multidimensional. Talking seriously about racism matters as much as acknowledging that white supremacy has its own rage and power that is insidious. The projection of a white racial shadow does not claim anything but privilege—ignorance of black suffering, ignorance of how to heal, ignorance of where to look within the self for self-healing that helps everyone else. This is what has to change. Healing comes because we can identify the poison. This poison is partly the projected fears and anxieties that fall onto an Africanist Other. This is the shadow of a white cultural racial complex that feels the experience of what Jung called the "irritant" under the skin. He says that blacks gets under the skin of whites. If this is true then they have learned to soothe their discomfort by increasing their power and through control of every aspect of our human lives. Their rage could be changing form because over the last 50 years the economic and social gains of African Americans has been cause for the rage to transform aided by politics.

Is a white cultural racial complex any better able to keep its power because of its unconscious *and* lived reality of the "supremacy of white"?

A difference between white and black racial complexes is that the former when emerging can have the subtleness born of centuries of understanding how to use its power in all the best and correct ways and places. An emerging cultural black racial complex, with whatever emotional tone accompanies it has historically, within the field of psychology been pronounced as pathologic. Not only a pathologic occurrence but one that should demand no empathetic attention.

I wonder if all the years of unconscious activity involving the complexes demand complete and *serious* attention to them in order for us to begin even the most minimal conversation. Does the white cultural complex, secured by centuries of a sense of superiority—a superiority complex also through association, lack motivation? Is its emotion that of complacency?

What is the *so-called trauma* of a white cultural racial complex?

Jungian psychology has been accepted into the American collective by sufficient numbers to provide clinical practices for hundreds of analysts and psychotherapists. The business practice of psychology has consistently grown and provided psycho-logical support for individuals, groups as well as large-scale organization. There are specializations for all sorts of issues and problems. The one issue which I have attempted to bring more out of shadow into the light is the one that deals with racism. The connection between the shadow and the racial complex has I believe kept us away from having healing, valuable discussions and peaceful considerations on how we can bring consciousness to our lives.

The cultural healing that is required for Africanist people has been a very long time in coming. It is still not here and will probably not be for still a longer while. Everyone will not be willing, desirous of caring about the centuries old trauma of African Americans. This is important to remember. Those who can will be atten-tive to their own pain and those within their cultural kinship. Cultural differences exist and I do believe Jung saw this and understood this difference in a way that American generally and Jungian psychology in particular has been unwilling to see.

However, if we can just see our way to increasing our awareness regarding a racial complex as we have to all the other complexes we have come to learn about over the years, I think that we will have moved deeper into an understanding of our human as well as our divine selves. Ego, the personal unconscious, and archetype will have found a place to mirror one another in a place of healing, turning from shadow towards the light.

CLOSING REFLECTIONS

I first became interested in the subject of psychological complexes soon after entering my training to become a Jungian analyst. Prior to this, even though I had experienced different types of psychotherapy, I had not been introduced to the concept of a *complex* or its workings. The term became familiar to me once I began my analytical work as an analysand of Analytical Psychology, or Jungian psychology as it is also commonly known. Drawing from my own personal experience as a patient receiving psychoanalysis within a Jungian psychological frame, over time I have become more deeply curious and engaged with C.G. Jung's ideas regarding the complex. In 1934 Jung while engaged with his development of what was later to become his Word Association Test, discovered patterns of emotional behavior with his subjects. These reaction patterns were grouped in a select way that Jung believed were experiment subject's responses to the word stimuli he presented and that these reactions were *autonomous actions* originating from within the psyche.

My interest in theories of psychological complexes evolving from Jung's work is tailored by my desire to deepen my understanding of what complexes are and how they work to determine our human behaviors. This is not necessarily only in a general manner but rather in a specific way. This specificity has to do with looking to Jung's idea of a complex within the context of ethnicity, racial relations and racism.

Though it is not well known—I believe this is true even within the Jungian analytical community, Jung spoke directly about what he called Negro and white (American) complexes. The very important significance of him speaking in the most brief way of what I have come to term a *racial complex*, is that this racial concept has remained basically hidden from our American and specifically Jungian psychology field and area.

This is significant because the basis of much of Jungian psychology revolves and intersects with clinical therapeutic work that engages with complexes that capture both analyst and patient. No Jungian clinical work proceeds in any fashion without an understanding of psychological complexes.

I believe it is of value to see how Jung first defined this most essential part of Jungian clinical psychology. However, it is relevant to note that at the time Jung was developing his initial ideas regarding the unconscious and unconscious processes. In the same manner that our psyche and unconscious has so much that can be unknown to ego consciousness, it was the same way in terms of the fluidity of the unconscious. Our definitions must remain fluid and always in consideration of knowing how little we can ever *fully* know about unconscious processes. This is said with a great deal of respect for trusting the strength of the ego while having a willingness to always be an explorer, a nomad within the realm of the unconscious.

Jung says the following in *A Review of the Complex Theory* about which he first wrote and lectured in 1934, and this essay was later published as a part of his *Collected Works*, Volume 10.

In writing of the complex Jung states: "Today we can take it as moderately certain that complexes are in fact "splinter psyches." This allows us to understand that our behaviors, when influenced by a complex, have what Jung has defined as a "freedom." We do not have complexes—they in fact have us.

As we think about Jungian psychology we see how often we must consider the "smallness" of our own egos in favor of the much greater power of the unconscious as a whole. We can come to believe that the persona or the ego represents the fullness of how we define ourselves. Aging more into the life cycle, we may actually wake up to realizing that there is more to living than what the ego presents. I believe this is a basis for Jungian psychology. I also believe that having a deeper understanding of our unconscious processes—those that are relevant in Jungian clinical work, such as an understanding of archetypes, dreams and complexes, deepens the richness of the life. Some even believe that working within the realm of the unconscious with the energies of these aspects of Jungian clinical work allow us to have a spiritual life. We come to understand that having a strong ego for its purposes that remains basically food, shelter and clothing, and minor extensions of these—allowing for ego gratifications that can include learning, wealth, the fastest car, still can leave us emotionally unfulfilled. Our search in life is not only for the material but as aging continues, becomes a search for something much more meaningful. This is the place and time where we can become willing to dive further into an understanding of unconscious processes such as complexes.

When I first began my own personal clinical work in Analytical Psychology I had no idea regarding complexes. Gradually over time my analyst introduced me to personal complexes. In addition, I began more depthful reading of Jung's writings and that of other Jungian analytical writers. The experience of my own clinical work which brought me and my emotional self more inward also provided a new way in which to think of myself as being held by something other than that which was defined by ego alone.

In *The Racial Complex*, I hope to move Jung's initial theoretical ideas of the complex into a broader area that includes a cultural complex—specifically that of a *racial complex*. I think it is important to consider just the simple and yet very "complicated" idea of a complex. When Jung states as he does above, that complexes are splintered pieces broken off from our psyches, what does this mean? How can we think about his concept and this rather esoteric idea using language from the 19th century to help us clarify something that holds us, that is not entirely ego consciousness and that has fluidity like unseen particles of ion? This is both our challenge and oftentimes painful exploration as we delve into the psychological work of being with parental complexes, guilt complexes and others that we may know too well and yet not at all.

The writing of this book then is pointed towards listening to an inner voice that can address those places that generally are in shadow. Complexes are as Jung has called them "impish tricksters." This suggests a playfulness that can be present as we consider complexes. However, I want to take us further into the darkness of complexes as we bring light to the shadow of them as part of our collective consciousness.

In my discussion of complexes, I wish for us to look not just into the personal complex of raciality or ethnicity but also in the group racial cultural complex that binds us. This includes viewing the Shadow archetype that I suggest exist as a core feature of the racial complex. Analytical psychology suggests that each complex has a core archetypal energy that promotes its influence on the complex itself. I think that the Shadow archetype is this place of the core of the racial complex.

I understand that even the suggestion of a racial complex might raise serious questions and doubt as to the existence of such a complex. There are ways in which I follow Jung's lead and ways in which we separate. I have previously spoken of two major ways through previous writings (Brewster, 2017). I believe it is important to attempt to decipher psychological information provided to us by those who have contributed a great deal to the field of psychology. I also believe that Jung has made contributions—which oftentimes have been dismissed, in discussions within our field of psychology. I believe Jung when he has proposed and many times inspired us to follow our dreams, follow our myth—basically follow our passion. One of my passions is trying to fall into a deeper consciousness that gives information towards our psychological healing as a collective. When I am able to follow in a discriminating way, Jung's lead in selected ideas, I hope that this allows me to make a contribution to our collective psychological wellness.

Jung spoke of what I have titled the racial complex long before others were addressing this within the field of psychology. The very few historical writings from the early years of American psychoanalysis where others spoke of a *color complex* were discussed.

In the same way in which I follow Jung's lead in a furthering of our attention being brought to the complex, I hope to further his initial idea of the complex through a Jungian lens that is willing to see and provide increased clarity into racial relations and multicultural ethnic collective issues involving racism. Jung believed that our complexes—those fragmented parts of our psyche—became split off due to what he called a "so call trauma."

When I explore our collective social and psychological issues of racism I wonder how many of these issues are due to unresolved personal and collective cultural racial complexes. *The Racial Complex* explores cultural trauma, the paradox of racism, the racial complex in American cinema, and other areas of realized psychological distress. These areas of distress are related to race and racism in our society. I wish to see if by following Jung in his theoretical foundation laid by his complex theory we might find an enhanced way of seeing into and through our society racial problems. Perhaps there is a way having previously unspoken language—racial complex, can better our understanding of how we are functioning on an unconscious level. We may find that exploring our negatively racially driven behaviors—anger, hate, even murder—are deeply connected to the activation of racial complexes. I propose this as a continuation of the thoughtful thread laid out by Jung one hundred years ago. I find no reason not to pick up this thread and begin to weave and add more color and detail to what he proposed in 1934.

Jungian psychology has spread its psychological seeds into the American psychic earth.

We may not know very much about Jung's Theory of Opposites but we can feel emotional oppositional tension within ourselves and when we are in disagreement with others. We seek and know the release of this tension whether it is through the inner calmness that follows great psychological suffering or the release of pressure through harming or not harming another.

I have written *The Racial Complex: A Jungian Perspective* on *Culture and Race* because I want to extend Jung's work that he initially began one hundred years ago and see where we can find our psychological selves in the 21st century. Doing this addresses my passion and intention for wanting to see a shift in consciousness that can allow us as a collective to go beyond skin color, tribal impulses and racism, acknowledging differences while enriching our consciousness because of these differences. My writer's goals are personal, altruistic and hopeful. One of the main tenets of Jungian psychology is that we must be willing to experience all that causes us to be human. This includes every suffering, every pessimism, as well as every desire for what hope can bring. In this book I discussed the almost existential paradox of racism as well as an authentic possibility for racial healing. I do not have simple answers to the complicated questions in which we are presently engaged. I may only have more questions—the same as you, and I ask them in the faith that we can see a path to deeper psychological endurance and hope for our next one hundred years.

BIBLIOGRAPHY

Adams, M.V. (1996). *The Multicultural Imagination: "Race," Color, and the Unconscious.* London and New York: Routledge.

Anderson, C. (2016). *White Rage: The Unspoken Truth of Our Racial Divide.* New York: Bloomsbury Publishing.

Berg, A. (2014). "Engagement with the Other: Reflections from Post-Apartheid South Africa," *Confronting Cultural Trauma: Jungian Approaches to Understanding and Healing,* G. Gudaite and S. Murray (eds.). New Orleans, LA: Spring Journal Books.

Brewster, F. (2015). "The Derby," *Evening Street Review,* Number 13, Autumn 2015. Columbus, OH: Evening Street Press.

Brewster, F. (2017). *African Americans and Jungian Psychology: Leaving the Shadows.* London and New York: Routledge.

Brewster, F. *Archetypal Grief: Slavery's Legacy of Intergenerational Child Loss.* London New York Routledge.

Bynum, E.B. (2012). *The African Unconscious: Roots of Ancient Mysticism and Modern Psychology.* New York: Cosimo Books.

Carmichael, S. (2001). "Black Power: The Politics of Liberation in America," *Racism: Essential Readings,* E. Cashmore and J. Jennings (eds.). London: SAGE, pp. 111–122.

Carotenuto, A. (1991). *Kant's Dove: The History of Transference in Psychoanalysis.* Wilmette, IL: Chiron Publications.

Corbett, L. (1997). *The Religious Function of the Psyche.* London and New York: Routledge.

DeGruy, J. (2005). *Post Traumatic Slave Syndrome: America's Legacy of Enduring Injury and Healing.* Portland, OR: Joy DeGruy Publications.

Dieckmann, H. (1999). *Complexes: Diagnosis and Therapy in Analytical Psychology.* Wilmette, IL: Chiron Publications.

Duran, E. (2006). *Healing the Soul Wound: Counseling with American Indians and Other Native Peoples.* New York and London. Teachers College Press.

Eyerman, R. (2001). *Cultural Trauma: Slavery and the Formation of African American Identity.* New York: Cambridge University Press.

Fletchman Smith, B. (2011). *Transcending the Legacies of Slavery: A Psychoanalytic View.* London: Karnac Books.

Fontelieu, S. (2018). *The Archetypal Pan in America: Hypermasculinity and Terror.* London and New York: Routledge.

Franklin, J.A., (1997). *From Slavery to Freedom: A History of African Americans* (7th ed.) New York: McGraw-Hill College.

Gates, H. and McKay, N. (2004). *The Norton Anthology of African American Literature* (2nd edition). New York and London: Norton & Company.

Grier, W.H. and Cobbs, P.M. (1968). *Black Rage.* New York: Harper Collins Publishers.

Gudaite, G. and Stein, M. (2014). "Engagement with the Other: Reflections from Post-Apartheid South Africa," *Confronting Cultural Trauma: Jungian Approaches to Understanding and Healing.* New Orleans, LA: Spring Journal Books, pp. 47–59.

Guthrie, R. (2004). *Even the Rat was White: A Historical View of Psychology.* Boston: Pearson Education.

Henderson, J. (1984). *Cultural Attitudes in Psychological Perspective.* Toronto: Inner City Books.

Herskovits, M.J. (1958). *The Myth of the Negro Past.* Boston: Beacon Press.

Hill, J. (2014). *Confronting Cultural Trauma.* New Orleans, LA: Spring Journal Books.

hooks, b. (1995). *Killing Rage: Ending Racism.* New York: Henry Holt and Company.

Iacoboni, M. (2009). *Mirroring People: The Science of Empathy and How We Connect with Others.* New York: Farrar, Straus and Giroux.

Jacobi, J. (1974). *Complex/Archetype/Symbol in the Psychology of C.G. Jung.* New York: Princeton University Press.

Johnson, A.G. (2006). *Privilege, Power, and Difference.* New York: McGraw Hill.

Joyce, J. (1996) *Ijala: Sonia Sanchez and the African Poetic Tradition* Chicago: Third World Press.

Jung, C.G. (1960/1981). *Collected Works,* vol. 8:*The Structure and Dynamics of the Psyche* (2nd edition). Trans.R.F.C. Hull. Princeton, NJ: Princeton University Press.

Kendi, I.X. (2016). *Stamped from the Beginning: The Definitive History of Racist Ideas in America.* New York: Nation Books.

Kimbles, S.L. (2014). *Phantom Narratives: The Unseen Contributions of Culture to Psyche.* Lanham, MD: Rowman & Littlefield.

Kirsch, J. (1995). "Transference," *Jungian Analysis* (2nd ed., M. Stein, ed.). Chicago and La Salle, IL: Open Court, pp. 170–209.

Kuhl, S. (2002). *The Nazi Connection: Eugenics, American Racism, and German National Socialism.* New York: Oxford University Press.

Levine, L. (2007). *Black Culture and Black Consciousness: Afro-American Folk Thought from Slavery to Freedom.* New York: Oxford University Press.

Levy-Bruhl, L. (1960). *How Natives Think.* New York: Washington Square Press.

Lind, J.E. (1914). "The Color Complex in the Negro," *Psychoanalytic Review,* 1, 4: 404–414.

Machtiger, H.G. (1995). "Countertransference," *Jungian Analysis* (2nd ed., M. Stein, ed.). Chicago and La Salle, IL: Open Court, p. 210.

Maher, M.J. (2012). *Racism and Cultural Diversity: Cultivating Racial Harmony through Counselling, Group Analysis, and Psychotherapy.* London: Karnac Books.

MalcolmX. (1971). *The End of White World Supremacy: Four Speeches by Malcolm X,* ImamB. Karim (ed.). New York: Arcade Publishing.

May, R. (1977). *The Meaning of Anxiety.* New York: W. W. Norton & Company.

Mayes, C. (2016). *An Introduction to the Collected Works of C.G. Jung: Psyche as Spirit.* Lanham, MD: Rowman & Littlefield.

Mbiti, J. (1989). *African Religion and Philosophy* (2nd ed). Portsmouth, NH: Heinemann.

Menakem, R. (2017). *My Mother's Hands: Racialized Trauma and the Pathway to Mending Our hearts and Bodies*. Las Vegas: Central Recovery Press.

Meyers, J.M. (2009). "Theoretical and Conceptual Approaches to African and African Psychology," *Handbook of African American Psychology*, H.A. Neville, B.M. Tynes, and S.O. Utsey (eds.). Thousand Oaks, CA: SAGE.

Moore, D.S. (2015). *The Developing Genome: An Introduction to Behavioral Epigenetics*. New York: Oxford University Press.

Morrison, T. (2017). *The Origin of Others*. Cambridge, MA: Harvard University Press.

Neville, H., Tynes, B., and Utsey, S. (2009). *Handbook of African American Psychology*. Los Angeles: SAGE Publications.

Panksepp, J. and Biven, L. (2012). *The Archeology of Mind: Neuroevolutionary Origins of Human Emotions*. New York and London: W. W. Norton & Company.

Rizzolatti, G. and Sinigaglia, C. (2008). *Mirrors in the Brain: How Our Minds Share Actions and Emotions*. New York: Oxford University Press.

Samuels, A. (1985). *Jung and the Post-Jungians*. London and New York: Routledge.

Samuels, A. (1986). *A Critical Dictionary of Jungian Analysis*. London and New York: Routledge.

Samuels, A. (2006). "Transference/countertransference," *The Handbook of Jungian Psychology: Theory, Practice and Applications*, R.K. Papadopoulos (ed.). London and New York: Routledge.

Shalit, E. (2002). *The Complex: Path of Transformation from Archetype to Ego*. Toronto: Inner City Books.

Shamdasani, S. (2003). *Jung and the Making of Modern Psychology: The Dream of a Science*. Cambridge: Cambridge University Press.

Shorter-Gooden, K. and Jackson, L. (2000). "The Interweaving of Cultural and Intrapsychic Issues in the Therapeutic Relationship," *Psychotherapy with African American Women: Innovations in Psychodynamic Perspectives and Practice*. New York: Guilford Press.

Snowden, F.M. (1997). *Before Color Prejudice: The Ancient View of Blacks*. Cambridge, MA: Harvard University Press.

Stein, M. (1995). *Encountering Jung on Evil*. Princeton, NJ: Princeton University Press.

Stein, M. (2010). *Jung's Map of the Soul: An Introduction*. Chicago and La Salle, IL: Open Court.

Stetson, E. (1981). *Black Sister: Poetry by Black American Women, 1746–1980*. Bloomington, IN: Indiana University Press.

Sublette, N. and Sublette, C. (2016). *The American Slave Coast: A History of the Slave-Breeding Industry*. Chicago: Lawrence Hill Books.

Takaki, R. (2008). *A Different Mirror: A History of Multiculturalism in America*. New York: Little, Brown, and Company.

Ulanov, A.B. (2003). "Scapegoating: The Double Cross," *Jung and the Shadow of Anti-Semitism*, A. Maidenbaum (ed.). Berwick, ME: Nicolas-Hays, Inc., pp. 97–112.

Washington, H. (2008). *Medical Apartheid: The Dark History of Medical Experimentation on Black Americans from Colonial Times to the Present*. New York: Random House.

Watkins, M. and Shulman, H. (2008). *Toward Psychologies of Liberation*. New York: Palgrave Macmillan.

Weisstub, E. (2000). "Reflections from the Back Side of a Dollar: Myths and the Origins of Diversity," *The Vision Thing: Myth, Politics and Psyche in the World*, T. Singer (ed.). London and New York: Routledge, chapter 9, p. 141.

White, J. and Parham, T. (1990). *The Psychology of Blacks*. Englewood Cliffs, NJ: Prentice-Hall.

Williams, C. (1987). *The Destruction of Black Civilization: Great Issues of a Race from 4500 B.C. to 2000 A.D.* Chicago: Third World Press.

INDEX

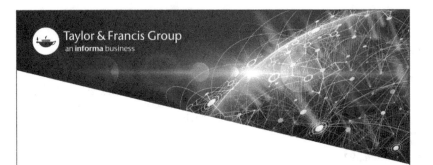